I Almost Died

Kimberly Moses And Co-Authors

Copyright © 2020 by Kimberly Moses And Co-Authors

All rights reserved. No part of this publication may be reproduced, distributed or transmitted in any form or by any means, including photocopying, recording, or other electronic or mechanical methods, without the prior written permission of the publisher, except in the case of brief quotations embodied in critical reviews and certain other noncommercial uses permitted by copyright law. For permission requests, write to the publisher, addressed "Attention: Permissions Coordinator," at the address below.

Kimberly Moses And Co-Authors/Rejoice Essential Publishing
PO BOX 512
Effingham, SC 29541
www.republishing.org

Unless otherwise indicated, scriptures are taken from the King James Version.

The Holy Bible, English Standard Version® (ESV®) Copyright © 2001 by Crossway, a publishing ministry of Good News Publishers. All rights reserved. ESV Text Edition: 2016

Scripture quotations marked (NIV) are taken from the Holy Bible, New International Version®, NIV®. Copyright © 1973, 1978, 1984, 2011 by Biblica, Inc.™ Used by permission of Zondervan. All rights reserved worldwide. www.zondervan.comThe "NIV" and "New International Version" are trademarks registered in the United States Patent and Trademark Office by Biblica, Inc.™

Scripture taken from the New King James Version®. Copyright © 1982 by Thomas Nelson. Used by permission. All rights reserved.

The Holy Bible: International Standard Version. Release 2.0, Build 2015.02.09. Copyright © 1995-2014 by ISV Foundation. ALL RIGHTS RESERVED INTERNATIONALLY. Used by permission of Davidson Press, LLC.

I Almost Died/Kimberly Moses And Co-Authors
ISBN-13: 978-1-952312-19-9

Dedication

This book wouldn't be possible without the inspiration of the Holy Spirit. He is the orignator of all ideas of each book collaboration. This manuscript took months to release and had warfare surrounding it.

2 Timothy 3:16-17 says, "All Scripture is given by inspiration of God, and is profitable for doctrine, for reproof, for correction, for instruction in righteousness. That the man of God may be perfect, throughly furnished unto all good works."

Death is an appointment that we all shall encounter as we travel through the journey called life. But we never think that our encounter will befall us often in the journey. Travel with me as I share with you the many times that death came knocking at my door, but God intervened and saved me to be here to tell my story

— Jalonzo Samuels

***

My prayer is that you would take account of the urgency of knowing where you will spend eternity. May it cause you to re-examine all the things you may or may not have known about Hell and why God created it. Let these words penetrate your hearts and mind to seek God and grow in godliness.

—Stephanie Ham

Table of Contents

ACKNOWLEDGEMENTS..xiii

PART ONE: Foundation...............................xv

INTRODUCTION..1

CHAPTER 1:   Declarations To Cancel
              Death By Melissa Jackson............9

CHAPTER 2:   Lessons Of Famous Deaths
              By Treasa Brown And
              Kimberly Moses........................25

CHAPTER 3:   The Benefits Of Life
              By Emelia Adjei And
              Kimberly Moses........................32

CHAPTER 4:   The Different Ways To
              Die By Michelle Loatman..........40

CHAPTER 5:   What Is Death?
              By Jalonzo Samuels..................49

CHAPTER 6:   What Is Heaven Like?
              By Tijuana Killian....................54

CHAPTER 7:	What Is Hell? By Stephanie Ham........62
CHAPTER 8:	Why Value Life? By Allen Douglas-Brathwaite ...64
PART TWO:	Testimonials...............70
CHAPTER 9:	Anemia by Melissa Jackson........71
CHAPTER 10:	BIRTH By Jalonzo Samuels...................87
	Possible Death In the Womb By Tréasa Brown.......................89
CHAPTER 11:	Blood Clots By Michelle Loatman..................97
CHAPTER 12:	Brain Aneurysm By Allena Douglas...................107
CHAPTER 13:	CAR ACCIDENT By Jalonzo Samuels.................112 By Kimberly Moses..................115
CHAPTER 14:	CHOKING Near Death in the Kitchen By Tréasa Brown.....................127

CHAPTER 15:	Crib Death By Kimberly Moses.................132
CHAPTER 16:	DOMESTIC VIOLENCE By Stephanie Ham...................139 By Allena Douglas...................143
CHAPTER 17:	Drowning By Jalonzo Samuels.................151
CHAPTER 18:	Terrorized By Fibrods By Emelia Adjei 154
CHAPTER 19:	Flesh By Michelle Loatman...............160
CHAPTER 20:	GUN VIOLENCE By Kimberly Moses...................174 357 Magnum By Jalonzo Samuels.................184
CHAPTER 21:	Lupus/Stroke By Tijuana Killian...................187
CHAPTER 22:	Nightmare Spirits By Stephanie Ham....................195

CHAPTER 23:	Pulmonary Embolism By Stephanie Ham..................198
CHAPTER 24:	Deadly Snakes By Stephanie Ham..................200
CHAPTER 25:	SUICIDE By Kimberly Moses..................203
	By Allena Douglas..................213

ABOUT THE AUTHORS..................216

REFERENCES..................234

Acknowledgements

Thank you to my husband, Tron, for helping me with the podcasts, and allowing me to write often.

Thank you to all my co-authors and believing in the vision that God has given me. We make a great team.

Thank you to my parents, Greg and Oretha, Thank you to my sisters, Ashley, Briana, and Britney.

Thank you to my spiritual parents, the Edmonds.

— Kimberly Moses

***

I am thankful to God to be able to write on this project with prophetess Kimberly Moses and the anointed men and women of God on this project.

— Allena Douglas

***

I want to give all glory and honor to my personal Lord and Savior, Jesus Christ. I am blessed and humbled to serve a merciful God of grace and second chances, who has continued to protect and guide me.

I want to praise God for my grandmother Erma, my best friends Tira and Grace, my Pastors, Anthony and Glenda Bailey, the many intercessors, and prayer partners at my church, Word Alive Worship Center. I am truly thankful to God for placing them in my life. Their faith, obedience to God, prayers, encouragement, and holding me accountable, has been life-changing!

And last but not least, I give honor and praise to God for opening the door of divine connection to my spiritual midwife, my mentor, coach, and prayer partner, Prophetess Kimberly Moses.

— Michelle Loatman

Part One
Foundation

Introduction

It's not by chance that you are reading this book. Are you weary and running out of options? Do you feel misunderstood and alone? Is the pain unbearable? Do you want to die or feel like your time is almost up? Give this book a chance before you toss it on your shelf somewhere to collect dust because it was orchestrated by heaven to help you and your loved ones. This opportunity is a call to action. Now is the time to decide how you are going to live your life. Have you ever watched the news or saw what's trending on social media and felt heavy? The media often portrays bad news, which causes panic and fear. Here are some examples of some news reports:

- A seven-year-old kills his grandparents
- A worldwide pandemic of a deadly virus with no known cure such as Covid-19

- A shooter walked into a Sunday service and killed a dozen people
- A daycare worker shook the baby and the infant died
- A person went into Walmart and shot a bunch of people
- A major celebrity commits suicide
- A famous singer died from an overdose
- A tourist took a selfie on the cliff and falls to their death
- A person drove into the crowds and deliberately ran over people

Do these incidences sound familiar? These are some fabricated examples, but real stories of this manner have occurred. Rarely do we hear something good and uplifting. The world is fascinated with death, and many different cultures have dedicated days unto the dead. Some cultures burn candles, fast, send kites or balloons, offer food and drink to spirits, and communicate with the dead. During Halloween, people are dressing up as ghosts and skeletons.

In Mexico, they celebrate Día de Muertos (October 31 - November 2nd), which means the day of the dead. Cultures in Cambodia, Malaysia, Japan, China, and some Hindu countries participate in certain rituals to pay homage to their deceased ancestors.

Risky lifestyles cause people to die prematurely. It seems that the crimes are becoming more heinous, and morality is at an all-time low. People take their life for granted by breaking the laws that are in place for our safety. For instance, there are laws against drinking and driving, but people continue to do so.

It's not until someone is killed that they realize they are negligent. The same applies to texting and driving and falling asleep behind the wheel. Some people don't care about the rules or regulations. We see them driving way over the speed limit, driving recklessly during adverse weather, not washing their hands when they prepare other's food in public eateries, robbing others, killing innocent people, and the list continues.

James 4:14 (ESV) says, "You do not know what tomorrow will bring. What is your life? For you are a mist that appears for a little time and then vanishes."

It's disheartened that people are living life on the edge and allowing the devil to end their life too soon. Many of my peers that I went to school with are no longer here. Some tragically died while others got killed over drugs, money, or adultery. I have witnessed people eat themselves to death because they were greedy. Their doctors warned them to eat better and exercise, but they kept eating fatty and greasy foods and died from a stroke or heart attack. During my health career, some of my patients had advanced respiratory disease, COPD, and emphysema, but they continued to smoke. They could be short of breath but would manage to inhale their cigarettes or cigars. Another patient had cirrhosis of the liver and needed a liver transplant, but he continued to drink alcohol like a fish. He passed away at a young age.

People are dying without fulfilling their purpose in life, and then when they get on their deathbeds, they are full of regrets. They may say, "I should've done this or that."

I decided that enough was enough and I must stand up and address this issue. Let's value our lives and stop taking it for granted. When the Lord gave me this idea for this book, I was grieved by the number of tragedies that I see daily. I hope that you are encouraged and appreciate life as you read the testimonials featured inside. We will also cover the following:

1. What does the Bible say about death?

- We have gotten away from the standard of the Word of God. The Bible is the instructions we need to follow while living here on this earth.

2. Different ways to die

- You will be shocked at the many ways people have died.

3. Where will we spend eternity?

- Will your soul go to heaven or hell? Many people have tried to say that heaven and hell don't exist, but we will show you otherwise.

4. What is heaven or hell like?

- You will read bone-chilling testimonies from those who have experienced the afterworld firsthand.

5. Declarations to cancel death

- Do you feel that you or your loved ones may die prematurely? The best way to rebuke the spirit of death is by praying the Word of God.

6. Why do we need to value life?

- No one lives forever and there is an appointed time for each of us to die. During our time on earth, we need to make the best of it and make sure that we are in the right standing with the Lord.

7. The benefits of life

- The gift of life is valuable, and many people aren't fortunate to experience it. The Lord blesses us with family, friends, great opportunities, and the experience of walking in our purposes.

8. Lessons learned from famous deaths

- Whenever a celebrity dies, it can be shocking and impact a lot of people. We will discuss a few lessons learned as we reflected on what happened to them.

Before we move any further, an important topic must be discussed: salvation. Do you know where you are going when you leave this world? Do you know Jesus as your personal Lord and Savior? Do you need to rededicate your life to the Lord? Beloved, don't pass up this opportunity to accept the Lord Jesus in your heart. If you answered 'no' to the previous questions, then pray the following prayer out loud.

Dear God,

I come before You and repent of all my sins. I'm a sinner and I don't want to take the chance of dying one day without being in right standing with You. I'm tired of doing things my way and want to do things Your way. Romans 10:9 says, that if I confess with my mouth that Jesus is Lord and believe in my heart that God raised him from the dead, I will be saved. Jesus, I believe in you. Come into my heart today. Teach me how to follow You with my whole heart, soul, and mind. Thank You for answering this prayer. Amen.

If you prayed this prayer, welcome to the body of Christ. There are some steps that you must take to help you succeed.

1. Get a Bible and read it every day. If you don't understand it, pray before you read and ask the Lord for understanding.

2. Get water baptized because it's a part of the plan of salvation. After people received salvation in the Bible, they were water baptized immediately. Make sure that you are fully submerged in the water because it symbolizes the washing away of your sins and the resurrection of Jesus Christ.

1 Peter 3:21-22 (ESV) says, "Baptism, which corresponds to this, now saves you, not as a removal of dirt from the body but as an appeal to God for a good conscience, through the resurrection of Jesus Christ."

3. Pray to be filled with the Holy Spirit. The Holy Spirit is the Spirit of truth who will guide you into all truth (John 16:13). He will be a friend and will bless you with the strength to live uprightly before the Lord. After Jesus ascended, He sent the Holy Spirit, who is the third part of the Godhead: the Father, Son, and Holy Spirit.

John 16:7 (ESV) says, "Nevertheless, I tell you the truth: it is to your advantage that I go away, for if I do not go away, the Helper will not come to you. But if I go, I will send him to you."

4. Make sure you pray always so you won't be led into temptation (Matthew 26:41). The enemy will try to pull you back into your old life. Much prayer equals much power. A strong prayer life helps you resist the devil and submit to God.

5. Tell people that are negative influences in your life about your salvation. Separate yourself from them so they don't pull you back into sin and surround yourself with believers in the faith of Jesus Christ so they can encourage you and keep you accountable.

1 Corinthians 15:33 says, "Be not deceived: evil communications corrupt good manners."

Your life is about to change, and you are about to embark upon a new journey. After you finish this book, make sure that you pass it on to someone who is living a reckless life.

CHAPTER 1

Declarations To Cancel Death.

BY MELISSA JACKSON

I cancel death in my life by the living blood of the Lamb, Jesus Christ, the Son of God.

Thank you, Father, in the name of Jesus for your perfect plan for my life.

Thank you, Father, in the mighty name of Jesus for allowing me to have the breath of life.

Thank you, Jesus Christ, the Son of God, for making the Word flesh.

Thank you, Jesus, for listening to the Father to be the perfect example for us.

Knowing that Christ being raised from the dead dieth no more; death has no more dominion over Him. (Romans 6:9)

Thank you, Jesus, for dying for all my sins.

Thank you, Jesus, for teaching us how to use the power to cancel death.

Thank you, Father, for the blood of Jesus that covers all my sin and from the sting of death.

Thank you, Almighty God, for this life you have given to me.

Thank you for taking my sin on the cross and dying just for me.

Thank you, God, for forgiving my sins and iniquities.

Thank you, Lord, for divine protection.

Thank you, Father, in the name of Jesus for pointing me away from death.

I cancel death in my family in the name of Jesus.

I cancel premeditated death in the name of Jesus.

I cancel negligible death in the name of Jesus.

I denounce premature death in the name of Jesus.

Treasures of wickedness profits nothing: but righteousness delivereth from death. (Proverbs 10:2)

I cancel unrighteousness in my life and my family.

I cancel wickedness that causes death to have legal authority in my life in the name of Jesus.

I activate my assigned angels for full protection from death in the name of Jesus.

I repent of known and unknown sins in the name of Jesus.

I plead the blood of Jesus over my life.

I decree a protective hedge all around me by the blood of the Lamb.

I am he that liveth, and was dead; and behold, I am alive forevermore, amen; and have the keys of Hell and death. (Revelation 1:18)

Death cannot come near my dwelling in the name of Jesus.

I speak long life over me and my generations in the name of Jesus.

I cancel accidental death in the name of Jesus.

Thank you, Jesus, for setting me free from death.

I cancel death in my life in the name of Jesus.

I claim Proverbs 4:20-22 that says "My son, attend to my words; incline thine ear unto my sayings. Let them not depart from thine eyes; keep them in the midst of thine heart. For they are life unto those that find them, and health to all their flesh.

I cancel generational curses in the name of Jesus.

I decree and declare that generational death curses be removed from my family and me in the name of Jesus.

I cancel the demonic spirit of death over my life and my generations in the name of Jesus.

I rebuke every demonic death spirit around my family and me in the name of Jesus.

Roman 6:23 states, "For the wages of sin is death; but the gift of God is eternal life through Jesus Christ our Lord."

Father, in the name of Jesus, I ask that You block sin from my life.

Father, please forgive me for speaking death over anyone's life in the name of Jesus.

Father, forgive me for speaking death over my life in the name of Jesus.

I cancel every word I spoke to let the spirit of death in my life in the name of Jesus.

Father, forgive me for not taking care of my body in the name of Jesus.

I declare that I will eat the right food to nourish my body.

I decree that I will take care of my organs in the name of Jesus.

The Word of God says, "For whoso findeth me findeth life, and shall obtain favour of the LORD." (Proverbs 8:35-36)

The fear of the LORD is the fountain of life and I shall avoid the captivities of death. (Proverbs 14:27)

I decree that I will be turned from the snares of death.

I declare that I am living life in the overflow in the name of Jesus.

I decree that I will find God to find life.

I plead the blood of Jesus over my life.

I cancel the enemy's plot to kill me in the name of Jesus.

I rebuke the plans of the enemy for my life in the mighty name of Jesus.

I decree a hedge all around me in the name of Jesus.

I denounce any words that are associated with an early death sentence in the name of Jesus.

No weapon formed against me shall prosper. (Isaiah 54:17)

I rebuke evil talk about my health in the name Jesus.

I rebuke demonic talk about my healing in the name of Jesus.

I rebuke every evil tongue that speaks against my faith to live and not die in the name of Jesus.

I bind up the mouths that speak of death over my life in the name of Jesus.

I cast out wicked tongues against me in the mighty name of Jesus.

I decree the favor of God on my life in the name of Jesus

I decree that ministering angels are all around me in the name of Jesus.

I decree that I will have life and life more abundantly.

But seek ye first the kingdom of God, and his righteousness; and all these things shall be added unto you." (Matthew 6:33)

I decree that I will seek the kingdom of God and all His righteousness, and all these things shall be added unto me.

The thief cometh not, but for to steal, and to kill, and to destroy: I am come that they might have life, and that they might have it more abundantly."(John 10:10)

I bind the enemy from trying to destroy me in the name of Jesus. The Lord rebukes the one that is seeking to devour me.

"Delight thyself also in the LORD; and he shall give thee the desires of thine heart. Ps 37:4

I decree that I will delight myself in the Word of God to experience life.

I decree my season of death is over in the name of Jesus.

I rebuke the thought of death in the name of Jesus.

I repent for opening portals of evil to enter my life.

I rebuke all spirits that influenced me to willingly open portals that would allow premature death in the name of Jesus.

I decree that sickness that causes death is over by the power of God.

I rebuke car accidents.

I rebuke accidents at work.

I cancel any unsafe thoughts in my heart.

I rebuke freak accidents in the name of Jesus.

I decree that the Lord thy God will rebuke all thoughts of suicide in me and around me.

I thank God for delivering me from evil thoughts.

I rebuke all evil spirits to be removed from around me by the blood of the Lamb.

I decree a hedge of protection all around me by the blood of Jesus.

I bind up evil spirits that will push me in the wrong mind frame. Father, I ask that you forgive me for opening portals that allowed the death spirit to be around me.

I bind up and cast out all evil materials around me that open portals.

I decree that I am walking in the abundance of life from this day on.

I bind self-neglect.

I cancel any distractions in the name of Jesus.

I cancel all thoughts that are not of God in the name of Jesus.

I bind demonic blockage in the name of Jesus.

I decree that I will not ignore warning signs/red flags in my body in the name of Jesus.

I decree that I am moving forward with the works of God for my life.

I cancel death to my calling and I am protected by the blood of the Lamb.

I bind up the fear of death in the name of Jesus.

I cast out the thoughts of death for family members and me in the name of Jesus.

I claim perfect love in my life that casts out all fear in the name of Jesus.

I SHALL LIVE and NOT DIE in the name of Jesus.

I shall enter into His gates with praise at all times.

I bind up people who try to take my blessing of life in the name of Jesus.

I claim that I will get the help that I need for my body to live for God.

I decree that I will rise up from my low place in the name of Jesus.

The second is this: 'Love your neighbor as yourself.' There is no commandment greater than these."

I decree that I will love myself.

I decree that I will listen to my body in the name of Jesus.

I decree I will take time out for myself daily.

I decree that I will get regular checkups in the name of Jesus.

I decree I will do what it takes to stay healthy.

I receive the will of God for my life to be prosperous.

I decree that I will take care of my mind with a positive atmosphere.

I repent for not taking care of my wonderfully made body God has given to me.

I repent for not loving my body in the name of Jesus.

I claim in the name of Jesus that I will pay attention to the symptoms of any dis-ease in my body.

I cancel anxiety when I feel disease in my body.

I decree that I will not procrastinate about my healing.

I denounce getting out of character when my body is not at ease in the name of Jesus.

I decree that I will not neglect the warning symptoms in my body in the name of Jesus.

I decree I will take care of my body with physical exercise to stay healthy.

I decree I will take care of my body with a proper diet in the name of Jesus.

I decree I will take care of my soul by reading the Word of God daily.

God is to us the God of deliverances. The Lord God rescues us from death. — Psalm 68:20 (ISV)

I decree full deliverance in my life.

I claim salvation in my life.

I choose to live in the name of Jesus.

I cancel death over my purpose in the name of Jesus.

I choose to have a sound mind in the name of Jesus.

I choose to walk in the power of Jesus.

I choose to live life abundantly in the name of Jesus.

I cancel living in lack in the name of Jesus.

I choose to live for God and do the calling on my life.

I cancel distractions in the name of Jesus.

I choose to LIVE.

I choose to LOVE.

I choose the Power of God to work in me.

I choose to believe in the words that the Holy Ghost speaks to me about my life.

What shall we then say to these things? If God be for us, who can be against us? (Romans 8:31)

I cancel any stress that tries to come my way.

I come against any situation that may trigger stress in my life.

I decree that I am covered by the Power of God.

I decree that nothing can come against me.

I declare that God is for me. Therefore, nothing has the authority to come against me.

I command the spirit of death to remove itself from around my dwelling in the name of Jesus.

I decree the Spirit of God to be all around me in the name of Jesus.

I plead the blood over my body in the name of Jesus.

I command every open door that allows discomfort in my life to be closed in the name of Jesus.

I cancel all witchcraft and demonic spirits attached to me to be removed, set on fire, and sent to hell in the name of Jesus.

I decree that no stress will take me out in the name of Jesus.

I loose myself from the plans of the enemy.

I decree that the spirit of death be revealed and dismissed in the name of Jesus.

I thank You for allowing me to praise You during the dark hours in the name of Jesus.

I thank You, Father, for Your perfect plan in Jesus name.

Thank You for making me a child of the Highest God and giving me the breath of life.

The blood of Jesus is against the spirit of death.

THE BLOOD of JESUS – THE BLOOD of JESUS – THE BLOOD OF JESUS still works.

I rebuke the spirit of the fear of death.

I cancel death over my co-workers in the name of Jesus.

I cancel death over my church members in the name of Jesus.

I cancel death over my mentor in the name of Jesus.

I cancel death over my leaders in the name of Jesus.

I claim Christ-like characteristics.

Jesus Christ said it and that settles it!!!

I will bless the Lord at all times.

I decree I will be a testimony.

I will trust in the Lord at all times and His words will be in my mouth.

I shall live and not die.

I cancel every evil assignment against me in the name of Jesus.

Who shall separate us from the love of Christ? Shall tribulation, or distress, or persecution, or famine, or nakedness, or peril, or sword? As it is written, for thy sake we are killed all the day long; we are accounted as sheep for the slaughter. Nay, in all these things we are more than conquerors through him that loved us. For I am persuaded, that neither death, nor life, nor angels, nor principalities, nor powers, nor things present, nor things to come, nor height, nor depth, nor any other creature, shall be able to separate us from the love of God, which is in Christ Jesus our Lord. (Romans 8:35-39)

I have a great knowledge that God still has work for me to do, so I must live in the name of Jesus.

Thank you for the love of the Father and making things all new!

Satan, the Lord thy God rebuke you!

Death, you are now canceled by the Power of the Blood of the Lamb, Christ Jesus the Son of the Most High God. Amen.

CHAPTER 2

Lessons Of Famous Deaths

BY TREASA BROWN AND KIMBERLY MOSES

There are many different people, celebrities, and leaders that have died, that we can learn lessons from. Let's look at three lives to gain a greater appreciation of life. The first example is Martin Luther King Jr., who came to mind right away! Dr. King was assassinated in Memphis, Tennessee, on April 4, 1968. According to the History Channel, he was fatally shot while standing on the balcony outside his second-story room at the Lorraine Motel. [1]He was a true pioneer of the Civil Rights Movement. His enemies were threatened by him, so they arrested

---

1. History.com Editors, Dr. Martin Luther King, Jr. is assassinated, History, https://www.history.com/this-day-in-history/dr-king-is-assassinated. January 30, 2020.

him and violated his privacy by tapping his phone calls and bugging his home. They were desperate to stop him because many people were encouraged to fight for equality, as he led protests. Dr. King stood his ground and continued to be a peacemaker despite the acts of violence and racism.

Matthew 5:9 says, "Blessed are the peacemakers for they shall be called the sons of God."

The enemy doesn't mess with 'nobodies.' When you are a threat to the kingdom of darkness, the devil will try all kinds of tactics to stop your progress. The devil wants to shut you down, but you must keep your peace because you represent Christ. When you hold your peace, the Lord will fight for you (Exodus 14:14). You can't give the enemy the satisfaction of a reaction. Dr. King set his face like a flint (Isaiah 50:7) because he was focused on his assignment.

He died with honor and seemingly fulfilled destiny and his purpose. He knew he was going to die young, but he died leaving an impact on the world! He had ambition, courage, leadership, and a drive that led us to our freedom. God gave him a purpose to fulfill. With the help of the Lord, he carried it out and it cost him his life! But he was willing to go all the way. He was all in! Dr. King made such an impact in the 20th century that he has been honored with his own day, January 20th. This day celebrates his life and legacy. It is a great reminder of the price that was paid for equality among different races.

What we can learn and discern in the spirit is don't die while pushing towards your destiny. Don't throw in the towel, don't give up and don't allow the enemy to steal your vision. Own it! Pursue it! Birth out your purpose while you are alive and well! The Bible tells us in Philippians 4:13, "I can do all things through Christ which strengthened me." Meaning there's NOTHING that we can't do without Him! Imagine what God will do through you when you walk in destiny.

The next example is Michael Jackson. One who left an impact as well on the world, but we know that he didn't do the work for the Kingdom of God. Michael Jackson was talented and a trend setter. His songs are still sung years after his demise. His dance moves are replicated as he is an idol to many celebrities and inspiring stars. In life, he struggled with self-esteem issues because he altered his appearance. Over the years, we can observe his complexion becoming lighter, his nose becoming slimmer, and his hair changing in texture. According to the LA Times, his sexual preferences was questioned when rumors surfaced of child molestation. He was investigated in 1993 by the Los Angeles Police Department.[2]

From the outside looking in, Michael seemed happy, but he was very depressed. He had fame, wealth, a huge mansion, and private amusement park in the pinnacle of his career. But Michael had a dark secret. For many years he suffered from insomnia. He was a user of strong sedatives or anesthetic to aid him to sleep. He often took propofol, which is a milky drug pumped into the veins. I remember watching the nurses administering it

---

2. Newton, John & Nazario, Susan. Police Say Seized Tapes Do No Incriminate Jackson: Investigation: Officials continue to interview children in connection with molestation allegations. LA Times, https://www.latimes.com/archives/la-xpm-1993-08-27-mn-28516-story.html. January 30, 2020

to prepare patients for intubation in the emergency room during my Respiratory Therapy career. Propofol helps one to relax and slows the heart rate. On June 25, 2009, Jackson overdosed on propofol given to him by Doctor Conrad Murray.[3]

Money can't buy you happiness. Just because it seems like you have everything together doesn't mean you are intact internally. You never truly know what someone is dealing with behind closed doors. Michael had an internal war going on in his mind that he didn't know how to combat. He turned to drugs and acted strangely at times. As believers, we can have a peace of mind and be content in whatever state we are in because the Holy Spirit comforts us (John 14:26). The Bible teaches us how to renew our minds (Romans 12:2) and to walk in total victory.

Michael left a legacy, but I was very sad when I think about where he is spending eternity. Imagine how many souls could've been led to Christ, had he used his gifts for the Kingdom. If I had to sum up a lesson in his death, it would be, only what you do for Christ will last! How you leave an impact matters. When the Father calls you home, what will people remember about you? Will they know that you died living for Jesus? Many know him as "The King of Pop!" But there's no evidence of what he did for Christ. This definitely gives us something to think about and it's not about the validation from man. All I want to hear the Lord say is, "Well done, thy good and faithful servant," when He calls me home. I want to leave here knowing that I pointed people back to Christ!

---

3. History.com Editors, "King of Pop" Michael Jackson dies at age 50, https://www.history.com/this-day-in-history/king-of-pop-michael-jackson-dies-at-age-50. January 30, 2020.

The last example of lessons learned from famous deaths is to observe the life and legacy of Kobe Bryant. Kobe was a talented professional basketball player. After High School, he signed a contract to play on the LA Lakers. He set many records, won many tournaments, and he was esteemed highly by his peers. Often, he was compared to Michael Jordan. His fans honored him around the world. Kobe had everything going for him. He had a beautiful wife and children. He was arrested and fell into a sex scandal in 2003.[4] He realized that he was on the verge of losing his family, so he promised to honor his marital vows. He retired in 2017 from his NBA career and focused more on his businesses and family.

However, on January 26, 2020, the world was shocked by his death. At first, I thought it was fake news circulating on the internet because occasionally, there are false reported deaths of celebrities. Unfortunately, what the world dreaded was true. Kobe Bryant, his 13-year-old daughter Gianna, the pilot, and their friends, died in a helicopter crash in Calabasas, CA in route to a basketball game. The weather was foggy that morning and flying conditions weren't ideal.

I can recall the gut-wrenching feeling of watching the video of the helicopter crash that was recorded by an onlooker. You could see the helicopter almost reaching its destination with some people they were meeting on the nearby ledge. Suddenly as the helicopter crossed over the valley, around the mountains,

---

4. SI Staff (December 23, 2003). "Bryant distracted, scared amid sex assault case". Sports Illustrated. Associated Press. Archived from the original on September 6, 2004. Retrieved February 25, 2007.

and over the hills, the engine stopped and spiraled out of control. It was a horrific scene as the helicopter tumbled and rolled in the sky. A few seconds later, it crashed, causing an explosion and instantly killing everyone inside.

Kobe Bryant, who was a celebrity, had the best of everything. There was nothing that money couldn't buy him. Yet, death is something that we all must meet one day. One thing the rich and the poor have in common is that we will all leave this world one day. I truly believe that if the pilot had waited for the skies to clear that day, then there wouldn't have been a tragedy. We must follow the rules and regulations that are set in place. Lives are valuable and can't be replaced. It is better to be delayed and spare lives than to arrive in a body bag or a casket.

The lesson is to be ready in all seasons to meet your maker. You never know when your time is up.

James 4:14 (ESV) says, "Yet you do not know what tomorrow will bring. What is your life? For you are a mist that appears for a little time and then vanishes."

Life is but a vapor because we are here today and gone tomorrow. Kobe was only 41 years old. His death was a tragedy. Life is short because we all have an appointed time to die (Ecclesiastes 3).

On the morning of his death, he went to a Catholic mass. He gave his life to the Lord. How many people die daily and never give their life to God? The answer is many. However, you don't have to be a part of the statistics. As we reflected on Kobe's life, it's important to be in right standing with God because death can creep up on anyone despite their status. Forgive people and let the small stuff go. Don't be bitter and miserable. Enjoy your life. Work hard in the process by achieving your goals.

CHAPTER 3

The Benefits Of Life

BY EMELIA ADJEI AND KIMBERLY MOSES

WHAT'S LIFE?

Life is the existence of an individual. Life is the "quality that distinguishes a vital and functional being from a dead body" (Webster Dictionary).[5]

GIFT OF LIFE

After speaking the earth into existence, God created man in His own image. Genesis 2:7 says, "Then the LORD God formed man from the dust of the ground and breathed into his nostrils the breath of life, and the man became a living being." Human

---

5. Merriam-Webster.com Dictionary, s.v. "life," accessed March 1, 2020, https://www.merriam-webster.com/dictionary/life.

beings have the breath of God, which is a valuable gift. On the contrary, death is losing the breath of life. It's imperative that life is lived on purpose and service to glorify the creator. There's the cliché that life is precious; therefore, should not be taken for granted.

People die every day, but God woke you up today. You get another chance today at life, which is an opportunity for God to do something great in your life. When you want to complain, look around. There is always someone who is worse than you. Some people don't have food, shelter, and are stricken with diseases. Yet, you are okay, and you can function even in your dysfunction. Count your blessings.

ASPECTS OF LIFE

There are two aspects of life, the physical and spiritual. Physical life is our presence and existence on the earth, daily routines such as waking up, eating, and doing chores. Spiritual life is the path that a person chooses to follow the response of God within. Let's focus on the spiritual life. What we do on earth determines where we will spend eternity. That means after we finish living on earth, we will begin life in another realm.[6]

BENEFITS OF LIFE

There are many promises in the Bible with living righteously, pursuit and honor. Life has many benefits to recreate, explore,

---

6. Corr, A. Kenneth. "What Does It Mean to Lead a Spiritual Life? A Christian Perspective," Explore Faith, 2002. Accessed March 2, 2020. http://www.explorefaith.org/steppingstones_SpiritualLife_Corr.htm

learn and become a soul winner for the kingdom. Let's further explore some of these benefits of life and others.

1. Recreation

Being alive gives man the ability to recreate. In Genesis 1:28, God commanded man to be fruitful and multiply by bringing forth an offspring to increase the human species. Man has been given the privilege to be caretakers of animals, plants and have control over living species. The ability to reproduce is one of the greatest benefits because you have an opportunity to pass down a legacy. Children are our inheritance and a gift from God. People spend thousands on fertility treatments, abortion, and for surrogates. When God opens your womb to give birth to a living being, you are fulfilling the command to be fruitful and multiply.

2. Exploring

Life is full of exploration – nature, cultures, food, countries. God's creation is beautiful. There are mountains, oceans, skies, architects, volcanos, and certain landmarks that radiate His glory. There are so many species of animals that we haven't laid eyes on before. The choice in foods around the globe is waiting for our palates. The ability to travel is life-changing; you will gain a greater appreciation for life and perhaps value your own culture.

3. Learning

One does not have to place themselves in a box but learn something new. With each generation, technology evolves, and we learn something new. When we look back in history, we are sometimes appalled by people's dangerous actions such as eating poisonous foods, hazardous work practices, and inhumane medical treatment. There are a lot of books and resources to become knowledgeable in a particular craft. Information awaits us through videos or via the internet. In some cultures, people are hindered by a lack of education due to the shortage of supplies, teachers, and their gender.

4. Soul Winning

Christians have to win souls for the Kingdom of God for unbelievers to be saved to have eternal life. "But for this purpose I have raised you up, to show you my power, so that my name may be proclaimed in all the earth."(Exodus 9:16 NIV). Having life is not to occupy space, but God has set an expectation and given human beings grace and power to witness and share the Word. If we don't share the gospel of Jesus Christ, then that blood is on our hands. One day we will have to give an account for the lack of evangelism. Many people complain about working with sinners, but they have to realize that God has them on their job to witness to them. We can't only preach to church folks or believers, but we need to preach to sinners as well.

5. Memories

In life, we get the opportunity to make memories with those we love. We can age, which is a blessing. We get to experience losing our baby teeth, grow taller, go through puberty, go to prom, dates, vacations, get married, have children, and watch them grow up. Then we can make new memories with our grand or great grandchildren. We should cherish each moment because we never know what tomorrow will bring. We can take photos, videos, and keep letters to keep these memories fresh in our minds.

6. Wisdom

In life, we go through various trials and we can learn from our mistakes to help others to succeed. We know the consequences and gained a different perspective. We don't want to see our loved ones suffering from bad decisions. As we age, we should be increasing in wisdom and knowledge. Jesus learned obedience through the things that He suffered, and the same principle applies to us. As we increase in wisdom, opportunities will arise for us to mentor others.

7. Work

We can look forward to getting our reward one day from the hard work that we put in every day. Some of us are fortunate to save up for retirement over the years, so during the senior years, we can enjoy our lives. Others can accumulate properties and various assets that they labored for throughout the years.

As we work hard, we gain a greater appreciation of the things we acquired. You will be amazed at how you started from rock bottom, but now you have something to show for your toil. Don't despise small beginnings.

8. Discovering Purpose

We are here for a reason and we must discover our purpose. Once we do, then we are fulfilled, and we can start a journey of service. Many people die without ever fulfilling their purpose. Don't let that be you. Others are frustrated because they aren't experiencing God's best. They know that they should be doing more but unable to figure out exactly what they need to do. God wants us to live a life of fulfillment by sacrificing His son Jesus for us. "I've come so that they may have life and have it abundantly" (John 10:10 NIV).

9. Rest

We all need refreshing because God created us to rest. He even rested on the seventh day. When we can do get proper sleep and take a break occasionally, from various tasks, then we allow our bodies to recuperate. Many people are burned out from stress and the cares of this life. However, one of the benefits of living is resting, refocusing, and then going forward again in the tasks set before us.

10. Family

One of the blessings and benefits of life is family. Some people are more fortunate than others in this department. However, God's will is for families to be blessed and prosperous because it's one of the first institutions that He created. No matter what we face, our families have our back because blood is thicker than water. Even if your biological family is present, you can have a new family in the body of Christ. God will surround you with people who love and want the best for you.

11. Freedom

Another benefit of life is to have the ability of freedom. Some people in different countries don't have this luxury that we take for granted. They are underneath an oppressive leader and can't express themselves when it comes to religion or academia. God gives us the ability to have free will meaning that we are given a choice on what to do. Jesus Christ died on the Christ for our deliverance, so we no longer must be bound by the devil.

Until we really know the benefits of life, then can life truly be lived fully to glorify God? One of my favorite poems about life sums up the benefits and intricacies of life.

Life is a challenge, meet it
Life is a gift, accept it
Life is a sorrow, overcome it
Life is a tragedy, face it
Life is a mystery, unfold it

Life is an opportunity, take it
Life is a promise, complete it
Life is a struggle, fight it
Life is a goal, achieve it
Life is love, love it
Life is adventurous, have fun
Life is a duty, perform it
Life is a game, outsmart it
Life is a beauty, praise it
Life is great, make something good of it
So life is a celebration, eat, laugh, and do meditation.

By Gurajas Singh Narula

CHAPTER 4

The Different Ways To Die

BY MICHELLE LOATMAN

- Keeping toxic people in your life
- Believing the naysayers
- Being happy later
- Chronically complaining
- Fasting without the wisdom and direction of the Holy Spirit
- Not valuing time
- Your flesh
- Sin
- Living in fear
- Failing to take personal responsibility

- Physically
1. (Jas. 2:26; Gen. 35:18)
2. This death is the SEPARATION of the INWARD man from OUTWARD man (cf. Eph. 3:16; II Cor. 4:16).
3. There is no escape from physical death except at the Rapture! Barring the Rapture in our lifetime, we will all die. There is no escape despite the amazing advancements by technology, science, and medicine.
4. Our BODY of flesh is the outward man that dies, corrupts and returns to dust (Job 34:15).
5. On the other hand, the SOUL is the inward man that is immortal and incorruptible. The BODY may be dead, but the SOUL is alive forevermore in heaven (II Cor.5:8) or hell (Luke 16:23).
6. No soul will sleep but the body will sleep instead! One may be dead physically but that is not the end of everything (Heb. 9:27).
7. The Bible teaches that the SOUL is ever alive and conscious even when the BODY is dead. We get a foretaste of physical death when we sleep and dream!

- Spiritually
1. Separation from God
2. (Isa.59:2; Eph. 2:1)
3. This death is the SEPARATION of man from God because of sin.

- The fall of Adam (Gen. 2:16-17).
1. One can be alive physically but dead spiritually (Matt. 8:22; I Tim. 5:6).

2. A lost person may have a live body, live soul but dead spirit!
3. The good news is that a sinner can still escape spiritual death and be spiritually resurrected (Eph. 2:5).
4. A man has a lifetime of opportunity to escape spiritual death.

- "Once I was alive apart from law; but when the commandment came, sin sprang to life and I died. (Romans 7:9)
- "But we had to celebrate and be glad, because this brother of yours was dead and is alive again; he was lost and is found." (Luke 15:32)

- The second death
1. The last judgment (Rev: 20:11-15)
2. This will take place AFTER the Millennium at the Great White Throne Judgment. Contrary to popular belief, the Last Judgment does not occur at the Second Coming of Christ but only after His literal 1000-year earthly reign (Rev. 20:5-6).
3. At the Last Judgment, the dead will be physically resurrected which means that their bodies will again reunite with their souls to face God – the Judge and give an account. The sea, grave, death, and hell itself will give up ALL the bodies and souls in them to be judged.
4. Notice that this second death is the casting of both BODY and SOUL into the Lake of Fire (Matt. 10:28).
5. The Bible teaches TWO hells – one below the earth which is temporary (Matt. 12:40; Acts 2:27, 31) and the other above the earth which is everlasting – the Lake of Fire

which was prepared for the devil and His angels (Matt. 25:41).
6. Hell, itself will be cast into the Lake of Fire (Rev. 20:14) along with those who will perish after the Last Judgment.
7. The final death results in the casting into the Lake of Fire of all the "rubbish of the universe" – Satan and his unholy angels, death, hell, sin, and sadly, all who died without repenting of their sins and rejected Christ as Lord & Saviour!
8. Conclusion: The Lake of Fire in its final state will be thick darkness (Jude 13), unquenchable fire, torment, suffering, plus worms (Mark 9:44-48). Friend, life is short, death is sure, sin is a curse, but Christ is the hope and cure (John 11:25). Do you have 100% assurance of salvation in Christ?

- Positional death
1. Identification with Christ in His deaths (Rom. 6:1-14; Col. 2:13; Col 3:13)

- Temporal death
1. (Romans 8:6,13; Eph. 5:14; 1 Tim. 5:6; James 1:15; Rev. 3:1, KJV)

- Operational death
1. No production in time (James 2:26, KJV)

- Sexual death
1. Inability to procreate (Romans 4:17-21; Hebrews 11:12, KJV)

- Eternal
1. (Luke 16:19-21; Ezek. 18:4)
2. This is the SEPARATION of the SOUL from the BODY and SPIRIT to be cast into hell. When the BODY dies, it returns to dust and the SPIRIT returns to God who gave it (Eccl. 12:7).
3. When the body dies, there is no more second chance of salvation for then the SOUL is lost and condemned forever and ever. It will be separated from God ETERNALLY! Unlike spiritual death, eternal death is irreversible!

- Dead to self
1. Matthew 16:24-25; Mark 8:34-35; Luke 9:23-24, 14:27, 17:33; John 12:25; Romans 6:11, NKJ)

- Emotionally
- Mentally
- Psychologically
- Economically
- Financially
- Car accident
- Suicide
1. Superimposition of the believer's will over God's will (Romans 8:38, 39, KJV)

- Homicide
- Stroke
- Heart disease
- Heart attack

- High cholesterol
- High blood pressure
- Flu
- Chronic lower respiratory disease
- Septicemia
- A Deep Vein Thrombosis blood clot
- A pulmonary embolism blood clot
- Pneumonia
- Neonatal preterm birth defects
- Tuberculosis
- Cancer
- Alzheimer disease
- Dementia disease
- HIV/AIDS
- Diarrheal disease
- Malaria
- Coronavirus
- Airborne diseases
- Chronic Obstructive Heart Disease
- Vaccines
- Lack of proper vaccines
- Violence
- Kidney failure
- Liver disease
- Brain injury
- Parkinson's disease
- Alcohol
- Drugs
- Malnourishment
- Dehydration

- Cirrhosis
- Diabetes
- Congenital anomalies
- Suffocation
- Oxygen starvation
- High temperature
- Chemical toxins in the body
- Physical damage
- Internal bleeding
- Blood disease
- Obesity
- Meningitis
- Head injury
- Bacterial infection
- Carbon Monoxide
- Drowning
- Boating or water sport accident
- Work-related accidents
- Food poisoning
- Chemical poisoning
- Natural causes
- Animal attacks
- Infections from animal attacks
- Trauma from animal attacks
- Hurricane
- Tornado
- Volcanic eruption
- Tsunami
- Earthquake
- Mudslide

- Falling or jumping from a building, cliff, etc.
- A fire
- Insect bites
- Reptile bites
- Terrorism
- Bombs/explosions
- Gas explosions
- War battles
- Aircraft failure
- Lightening
- Electrocution
- Lethal injection
- Salmonella infection
- Contact with venomous plants, insects, reptiles, etc.
- Multiple bee stings
- Anaphylactic shock
- Asthma attack
- During medical operations and procedures (emergency & routine)
- Childbirth
- Abortion
- Sepsis
- Premature death
- Genetic diseases
- Sickle Cell
- Chronic organ failure
- Failed organ transplant
- Lupus

7,8,9,10,11,12

7. Geggel, Laura (February 9, 2016) The Odds of Science. Live Science. February 15, 2020. Retrieved from: https://www.livescience.com/3780-odds-dying.html#deadlydiseases

8. Carteron, Nancy, MD. May 4, 2016. Lupus Outlook: How Does It Affect My Lifespan? Healthline. February 15, 2020. Retrieved from: http://www.healthline.com/health/lupus

9. Pastor, Buddy Dano. Anderson Bible Church. Death. The Bible Lists Seven Different Deaths. February 15, 2020. Retrieved from: www.divineviewpoint.com/death.pdf

10. Science Focus The Home of BBC Science Focus Magazine. February 15, 2020. Retrieved from: https://www.sciencefocus.com/science/how-many-ways-can-you-die/

11. Shola (2020) 7 Ways that People Actually Die Before They're Actually Dead. The Positivity Solution. Making Positivity the New Reality. February 15, 2020. Retrieved from: http://thepositivitysolution.com/7-ways-to-die/

12. Silver, Marc (December 18, 2014) NPR. Death Comes in Many Different Ways. And Some are a Bit Surprising. Goats and Soda Stories of Life in a Changing World. February 15, 2020. Retrieved from: https://www.npr.org/sections/goatsandsoda/2014/12/18/371486989/death-comes-in-many-different-ways-and-some-are-a-bit-surprising

CHAPTER FIVE

What Is Death?

BY JALONZO SAMUELS

We have been told that death is the absence of life, a total separation from life, but there is so much more to death than what we have been taught. Hebrews 2:14 teaches that death is the effect of sin, so let us do further research into the matter of death.

According to Genesis 2:17, God gave to man, who was created in His own image, the command not to eat of the tree of knowledge of good and evil. Added to this command was the warning that in the day that you eat thereof and disobey My commandment, thou shall surely die.

Though not exclusively, the first aspect of this reference is indicative of bodily death. Yet because death by no means came upon Adam and Eve on the day of their transgression, but took place hundreds of years later, the expression, "in the day that," must be conceived in a much wider and deeper sense.

Therefore, apart from physical death, Scripture speaks of a second type of death, spiritual death. This death is when an individual is very much alive physically, but dead spiritually. All of us were born into the earth spiritually dead due to the transgression of Adam. We were born separated from God. Adam and Eve died spiritually the very moment that they sinned. They became different beings than those God had originally created. They were now eternally separated from God spiritually, and therefore, physically they began to die as well. Humanity was now separated from God by nature.

Jesus said in John 5:24, "Very truly I tell you, anyone who hears My Word and believes Him who sent Me has eternal life, does not come under judgment, but has passed from death to life."

Not only did sin bring separation from God by nature, but made man hostile to Him. The Apostle Paul spoke of believers in this manner in Ephesians 2:1-3... "And He made alive who were dead in your trespasses and sins in which you once lived, following the course of this world, following the ruler of the power of the air, the spirit that is now at work among those who are disobedient. All of us once lived among them in the passions of our flesh, following the desires of flesh and senses and were by nature the children of wrath."

He also wrote so profoundly in Romans 7:9 concerning being spiritually dead, "Once I was alive apart from the law, but when the commandment came, sin sprang to life and I died."

The reason that we are all born spiritually dead has to do with sin. We received our fallen nature from our parents. After Adam and Eve disobeyed God and transgressed His command, the death sentence was pronounced upon all of humanity. Therefore, each of us comes into this world spiritually separated from God. We came into this world born spiritually dead.

In Romans 8:1-2, the Apostle Paul introduces us to the "Law of Sin and Death." He contrasts two laws: the law of the Spirit and the law of Sin and Death. The Law of the Spirit is the Kingdom Gospel or Good News of Jesus Christ, the message of New Life through faith in the Resurrected Christ. The Law of Sin and Death is the Old Testament Law of God. The Law is holy, just and good (Romans 7:12), but because we cannot keep God's law on our own, the result is only sin and death for those under the law.

Romans 7:5 explains the focus on the law as leading to sin and death: for when we were in the realm of the flesh, the sinful passions aroused by the law were at work in us, so that we bore fruit for death. In contrast, the "way" or law of the Spirit is noted in Romans 7:6-7 states: "But by dying to that which bound us, we have become free or released from the law so that we serve in the new way of the Spirit, and not in the old way of the written code." However, the Law defined sin and stirred up our natural rebellion against God's rules, resulting in sin and death. Romans 7:10-11 defines how sin and death are connected in the deception, which brought forth death. This death refers to spiritual separation from God. Shackled by our depraved nature, we naturally opposed the Law and we found that God's life-giving Word served only to sentence us to death. It is because of this that Paul can refer to the Law as the "law of sin and death."

The conclusion of Romans 7 shows the need of the Gospel to deliver us from the consequences of sin under the Law. The Apostle Paul wrote, "For in my inner being I delight in the Law of God's Law, but I see another law at work in me waging war against the law of my mind and making me a prisoner of the sin at work in me."

Therefore, death came unto us because of the fallen nature of humanity. Death in the sense of the word is a matter of our choice of obedience or disobedience to the things of God. We can no longer operate in this life from our own will or desires to become alive, but solely upon our total obedience to the grace and mercy of God. Our eternal separation from the things of God is paramount to our being committed to understanding the Kingdom principles of His will. Additionally, it is paramount to understand the purpose for our restoration, which He has given through the gift of Christ to humanity.

Romans 5:12 informs us that as in Adam, all men died, but through the gift of Christ (the Second Adam), all men have been made alive through Him.

We find that the Law of Spirit and Life has made us free from the Law of Sin and Death. So, what is death really all about from a Biblical standpoint? Can we still be saved and yet dying in our soul? God's Word tells us that the soul that sins shall surely die. Can we that are born again continue to live in death and live? Therefore, we know that death is a sentence that was passed down unto us by an act that placed the whole earth in turmoil and placed us into eternal separation from God. Scripture tells us that God designed humanity to live eternally in relationship with Him. He created the rest of the universe by a mere command: speaking stars, planets, and oceans into being. But when it came to man, God's involvement was much more direct and intimate. Through mankind's sin, death brought a major separation from God into the world, which was never His intent. The very word death can trigger images of darkness and fear, but God does not want us to live in fear or defeat. He wants us to live and die with the confidence that comes from knowing that we belong to the victorious risen King, who defeated death when He died on the cross and rose from the grave. More than that, the reality of death can point to the incredible hope we have in Christ. Every heartache and struggle on earth can draw us closer to our Savior, center us deeper in His truths, and motivate us to engage in transformative conversations with others. May we learn to say, "To live is Christ and to die is gain" (Philippians 1:21).

CHAPTER 6

What Is Heaven Like?

BY TIJUANA KILLIAN

"In the beginning God created the heavens and the earth."- Genesis 1:1

"When He looks at you, the glory of God is emulating through Him. I fell at His feet. The angel of the Lord fell down. And I saw His feet. All my life, I thought Jesus had scars. But the holes in His feet were this big. I could see the light shining through."— Jesse Duplantis

How is heaven? It seems that it will be a place full of angelic beings who worship the Lord around His throne. The presence of God or the glory will be felt constantly, and we get to witness Jesus walk around daily. Heaven will be a place of peace because in His presence is the fullness of joy (Psalm 16:11). It will also be a place full of light as on a bright sunny day because the glory of the Lord will radiate strongly.

ENOCH AND ELIJAH

Can we see heaven before we die? Yes. There have been many testimonials of people going there, and the things they have seen are in alignment with Scriptures. Let's look at two men who are now presently there. Enoch and Elijah were both supernaturally transported to heaven. The Bible says that Enoch walked in habitual fellowship with God for three hundred years. And in reverent fear and obedience, Enoch walked with God; and He was not found among men because God took him away to be home with him. (Genesis 5: 22-24)

Elijah was taken up to heaven as well. "When the Lord was about to take Elijah up to heaven in a whirlwind, Elijah and Elisha were on their way from Gilgal." (2 Kings 2:1) "As they were walking along and talking together, suddenly a chariot of fire and horses of fire appeared and separated the two of them, and Elijah went up to heaven in a whirlwind." (2 Kings 2:11) Enoch and Elijah never tasted physical death. They were both carried away to be with God in heaven. Their lifestyle, character, and devotion pleased God to the point of taking them to be with Him forever. Being in right standing with God and accepting His Son, Jesus Christ, can ensure that we receive the gift of eternal life. I hope to be with God in heaven eternally one day as well. Do you?

"That angel said, what are you looking for? I said, you don't have no shadow. He looked at me and said there's no shadows here. God is light in whom there's no darkness."—Jesse Duplantis

NO MORE SUFFERING

"He will wipe every tear from their eyes, and there will be no more death, or sorrow or crying or pain. All these things are gone forever."—Revelation 2:14

These promises sound wonderful. Heaven is a happy place. We go through many trials and tribulations, ups and downs, gains and losses in life. I have had my fair share of sorrow, crying, and pain. Maybe you can relate and are saying, "Preach it, sister!" There were times when I just wanted to throw in the towel. I was faced with heart-aching disappointment regularly. Tears of anger, confusion, and hurt burned my cheeks as they jumped out of my eyes. The pain of poverty and sickness gripped my body in an unbearable way. Not to mention experiencing the death of a loved one that has a way of choking your heart and making you stiff and speechless. Yet all these emotions will not compare to the overwhelming victory and glory we will have in Christ Jesus. What we are going through is only temporal.

"Yet what we suffer now is nothing compared to the glory he will reveal to us later."— Romans 8:18

"There are flowers that I have never seen on earth before. And fragrances that I never smelled. Gold that is gold but yet transparent. Gold that looks like Crystal, yet its gold."— Jesse Duplantis

Heaven sounds like a beautiful place. Flowers can cheer up others and represent love, beauty, and devotion. Gold can be symbolic of quality, courage, wisdom, strength, and glory. These representations are everything that the Lord stands for and God is strategic because the components of heaven have a significant meaning.

I WANT TO GO

"But everyone who calls on the name of the LORD will be saved."— Acts 2:21

As we discussed earlier, heaven is a beautiful, amazingly, breathtaking place that we don't want to miss. So how do we attain this place? The Bible tells us, "That if we confess with our mouths, that Jesus is Lord, and if we believe in our heart that God raised Jesus from the dead, we will be saved. We believe in our hearts, and so we are made right with God. And we confess with our mouths, and so we are saved." (Romans 10:9-10) In other words, just ask Jesus to come into your heart, believe that He rose from the dead, and pray out loud to receive salvation to get on the path that leads to heaven.

There was a time when I wasn't saved and didn't know I needed to be. I attended church regularly as a youth with my family, but I wasn't born again. I believed going to church made me acceptable to God. It didn't. God wanted more for me. At the tender age of twenty-one, I became pregnant and lost the baby. He was born still born. I was devastated. The hospital staff suggested I see a chaplain. I agreed to it, thinking in my mind, I sure need something. A woman chaplain entered my hospital room and shared the Gospel of Jesus Christ with me. She then asked me if I wanted Jesus. She came the day after I lost my baby. In that surreal moment, I felt at ground zero, like I had hit rock bottom, and was up under the floorboards. Looking for hope, I told her yes. She led me into prayer. I asked for forgiveness of my sins, confessed Jesus as Lord, and gave my life to following Jesus Christ. I am presently following Him today.

The Bible tells us that everyone who calls on the name of the Lord shall be saved. - Acts 2:21. Will you trust Him today? Will you embark on a relationship with the God who died for you? Will you confess Him as Lord? The Lord is patient with us, not wanting any to perish, but everyone to come to repentance. - 1 Peter 3:9. Will you repent and live with Him eternally in heaven?

"This Place is unreal, ladies and gentlemen you don't want to miss heaven."— Jesse Duplantis

In my Father's house are many mansions; if it were not so, I would have told you. I go to prepare a place for you. And if I go and prepare a place for you, I will come again and receive you for Myself; that where I am, there you may be also. (John 14:2-4)

God has a special place that is prepared for you in heaven. If you are suffering, the promise of having your own mansion is uplifting. Heaven is a wealthy place.

There shall be no night there: They need no lamp nor light of the sun, for the Lord gives them light. And they shall reign forever and ever. (Revelation 22:5)

Imagine how bright the glory of God is? It's so illuminating that the sun isn't needed and the light from God will never be quenched.

And God will wipe away every tear from their eyes; there shall be no more death, nor sorrow, nor crying. There shall be no more pain, for the former things have passed away. (Revelation 21:4)

The promise of no more pain is a blessing that we can look forward to as we spend eternal life with God. Many people suffer from emotional bondage due to the experiences they endured. However, in the presence of the Lord, we will receive healing and deliverance permanently.

For our dying bodies must be transformed into bodies that will never die; our mortal bodies must be transformed into immortal bodies. Then, even our dying bodies have been transformed into bodies that will never die, this scripture still being fulfilled: "Death is swallowed up in victory. O Death, where is your victory? O Death, where is your sting?" (1 Corinthians 15:53-55)

If you are sick and dealing with afflictions in your body, then when you get to heaven, you will get a new one. That includes new organs, tissues, limbs, and anything else that was damaged.

You can enter God's Kingdom only through the narrow gate. The highway to hell is broad, and it's gate is wide for the many who choose that way. But the gateway to life is very narrow and the road is difficult, only a few ever find it. (Matthew 7:13-14)

You can't enter Heaven by following the way of the world because that route leads to eternal damnation. The world is contrary to the things of God (Romans 8). The world didn't know Jesus and didn't receive Him when He came, so they ended up crucifying Him. However, if you stay on the 'Holiness Highway', then you will stay on the narrow path.

Therefore, He is able, once and forever, to save those who come to God through Him. He lives forever to intercede with God on their behalf. (Hebrews 7:25)

Jesus will pray for you forever because He makes intercession on your behalf.

There is salvation in no one else! God has given no other name under heaven by which we must be saved. (Acts 4:12)

There are many false teachings about alternate ways to Heaven. Don't be deceived. Jesus is the only way to enter Heaven which is a gloriously beautiful place to spend eternity.

CHAPTER 7

What Is Hell?

BY STEPHANIE HAM

NAMES OF HELL:
- Sheol
- Underworld
- Gehenna
- Hades
- The Lake of Fire

The Oxford Dictionary translation gives the Hebrew and Greek meaning of Hell. For instance, in Hebrew, its Sheol, which means a place to depart. The Greek words are Hades or Gehenna, which happens to be a place for punishment for the wicked after death.

When I did some more research on the word Hell, I noticed that the Anchor Yale Bible Dictionary[13] quotes the Greek word Hades (hạdēs) is sometimes misleadingly translated "hell" in English versions of the New Testament (NT). It is referred to as the place of the dead but not necessarily a place of torment for the wicked. In Greek mythology, Hades was thought to be the god of the underworld. But more commonly, the term referred to his realm, the underworld, where the shades or the souls of the dead led a shadowy existence, hardly conscious and without memory of their former life. While Greek ideas about the afterlife probably did not influence the origins of Jewish expectations of retribution after death, later Jewish writers sometimes incorporated particular terms and concepts from the Greek and Roman Hades into their own pictures of the afterlife.

The old Hebrew concept of the place of the dead, most often called Sheol (šĕ◌ôl) in the Hebrew Bible, corresponded quite closely to the Greek Hades. Both were versions of the common ancient view of the underworld. Like the old Greek Hades, Sheol in the Hebrew Bible is the common fate of all the dead, a place of darkness and gloom, where the shades lead an unenviable, fading existence. In the LXX, therefore, Sheol is usually translated as Hades, and the Greek term was naturally and commonly used by Jews writing in Greek. This Jewish usage explains the ten NT occurrences of the word Hades.

---

13. Bauckham, R. (1992). Hades, Hell. In D. N. Freedman (Ed.), The Anchor Yale Bible Dictionary (Vol. 3, p. 14). New York: Doubleday.

CHAPTER 8

Why Value Life

BY ALLEN DOUGLAS-BRATHWAITE

God created the universe and decided to make man in His own image. He created the world for us to live in harmony with Him. Then God said, "Let us make man in our image, after our likeness." (Gen 1:26) God is the creator of all life forms: humans and animals. We should be honored and in awe. As God marveled about His creation of man, He graciously made woman as a help meet to man. God blessed Adam and Eve by setting them apart from all other forms of life and gave them dominion over every living thing. "Be fruitful and multiply and fill the earth and subdue it and have dominion over the fish of the sea and over the birds of the heavens and over every living thing that moves on the earth." When God saw everything that He made, He viewed that everything was good.

Even though Adam and Eve sinned against God, the world changed, but He still extended grace and mercy. There were instances of violence and continuous sin. Genesis 6:11 says, "The earth was corrupt in God's sight, and the earth was filled with violence." God sent a flood as a way of judgment. However, the world didn't change. After the flood, God gave humanity special protection.

And for your lifeblood I will require a reckoning: from every beast I will require it and from man. From his fellow man I will require a reckoning for the life of man. "'Whoever sheds the blood of man, by man shall his blood be shed, for God made man in his own image?"—Genesis 9:5-6 (ESV)

GRACE AND MERCY:

Grace is one of God's most important gifts and has been given to man repeatedly. The first evidence of grace was when God gave His only begotten Son to die for our sins. Jesus did not deserve to die upon the cross so many years ago because He was blameless and had not sinned. He was given as the ultimate sacrifice.

Grace means that we get extended unmerited divine assistance from God. Grace is God's blessing us despite the fact we don't deserve it. Mercy is when a person does not get what they deserve. In other words, God spares us from the punishment that should be merited. What a good God we serve. God is the only one that can give us grace. Mercy is to be given by both

God and man. Grace is God extending kindness, while mercy is deliverance from the judgment of sin. I value life because God continues to give grace and mercy and I have been a constant recipient of it.

We should value life when we see the splinters of His work. When you look out every day and see the beauty of the heavens, the mold in the stars, the trees to oceans, and the creation of our families, we should thank God because without the ultimate sacrifice, we will not be here (Psalms 8:1-9).

Despite sin, it is amazing that God is so great, and man is so small that He still values human life. We should appreciate life because Christ took our place for us to be forgiven, counted righteous, and restored to fellowship with God. Hallelujah!

I value life because I have been given a choice to be apart God's plan for redemption and restoration from the guilt of condemnation and sin. 1 Peter 2:9 states, "But ye are a chosen generation, a royal priesthood, an holy nation, a peculiar people, that ye should shew forth the praises of him who hath called you out of darkness into his marvelous light."

In our society, people don't value life because they don't know God or respect Him. God never said that life would be easy. But He provided us with instruction from the Bible and the Holy Spirit. God left it up to mankind to freely accept Him even though we see violence, killing, suicide, wars, and natural disasters. Life is still valuable because God gave us life and it is our birthright. He warns us in John 10:10 that "the thief cometh not, but to steal, kill and to destroy. I am come that they may have life, and that they may have it abundantly." We must make a conscious decision as to whom we shall serve. We are capable of conscious relationships with God and fellowship with Him. We reflect God's glory because He made us.

Life can easily be given and taken away at any moment. All life is precious because it is a gift from God. God has given each man and woman the precious opportunity to do integrated achievements in the things that they do. God has given us the gift of creativity to do miraculous things. Without all of this, God could have destroyed the earth and it would cease to exist as we know it.

Life without God or not having a relationship with Him would result in unhappiness. I am hopeful because I know that God loved us, as evidenced by Jesus dying on the cross. At that moment, we were given victory from sin. Despite all, we can still live a life walking with God. Knowing that life is a gift, has helped me navigate even in my joys and pains. Despite adversity and pain, I have found my hopes and greatest lessons of strength because of Him. I find myself being more thankful for it all.

Many naysayers ask, "What's the point of living this life? We are going to die one day." That is true. Some ask, "Why live when the world is so bad and it's getting worse?" We see the economic issues, rising health crises and the diverse conflict throughout the world.

The ultimate evidence that God considers life good is that He chose to redeem human life. God sent His Son to take on our human nature. Jesus became like us in every way but sin, sharing in our weaknesses and mortality. He redeemed life from bondage and restored it blameless in the sight of God.

God's plan is not just to redeem us from the guilt and condemnation of sin, but to restore us. God is renewing us from within so that we can love Him and do His will. The life given by God has a very special meaning, a value in which people sometimes forget to be thankful for or they either regret it. Many students/adults believe and measure success by gaining worldly goods, put value in titles, and accolades from achievements. If you look at it from society's point of view, they believe people should be given value according to what they do and their positions. Society measures life by money and a good job. James 1:17 is often forgotten, which says, "Every good gift and every perfect gift is from above and comes down from the Father of lights, with whom there is no variableness neither shadow or turning."

Matthew 6:19-20 says, "Do not lay up for yourselves treasures upon earth, where moth, and rust doth corrupt and where thieves breakthrough and steal. But lay up for yourselves treasures in heaven where neither moth nor where thieves do not break or steal."

God will hold each person accountable. Each person is a steward and will be judged based on whether they have received the redemptive work in Christ Jesus (John 3:16-18). We will also be judged on what we have done with the life God entrusted to us.

God's promises are everlasting. Even though death is imminent, we still have something to look forward to. Even in death, we will be given an opportunity to be with God. Our souls will be freed from sin. There will be no more pain or suffering. We have the promises of the resurrection, and total redemption if our name is written in the Book of Life. It is exciting to know that we will be reunited with God and live in His image forever. We will exist beyond the touch of sin and death forever. We will be sinless and immortal beings. We expect to live forever in His resurrection glory.

Despite anything that we have encountered, we have hope in Him. I take comfort in God's promises that death isn't the end. John 11:25 says, "Jesus said I am the resurrection and the life, he that believeth in me, though he were dead yet shall he live."

My faith and commitment are to glorify and serve Him. I will continually attempt to reflect His love, mercy, and grace. My prayers are that my service is pleasing in His sight. My goal is not to judge, condemn, or persecute anyone.

I will leave you with this, Jeremiah 31:3, "The Lord hath appeared of old unto me, saying, Yes, I have loved thee with an everlasting love, therefore with lovingkindness have I drawn thee."

Part Two
Testimonials

CHAPTER 9

Anemia

BY MELISSA JACKSON

IRON DEFICIENCY ANEMIA (IDA)

What is Iron Deficiency Anemia (IDA)? It is a condition caused by having too little iron in the body. According to Miller JL. Iron deficiency anemia[14], five million adults in the United States are affected. Therefore, you are not alone. Let's get a better understanding of IDA with a biology flashback.

---

14 Miller L. Iron deficiency anemia: common and curable disease. Cold Spring Harb Perspect Med. 2012; a011866,

15

16

Iron is a vital nutrient that travels through the bloodstreams in your body and is a necessity for the production of red blood cells (RBC)[17], [18]. Iron is what binds oxygen to the hemoglobin[19]. The hemoglobin is the oxygen carrier of the RBC from the lungs to the tissues[20]. The iron is absorbed through digestion and released into your bloodstream where the transportation protein, transferrin (a protein responsible for transporting

---

15.. Photo 1: Normal Blood compared to Anemic Blood. https://sabeelhomeoclinic.com/what-is-anemia-symptoms-causes-diagnosis-and-homeopathic-treatment/ Accessed February 29, 2020

16. Photo 2: https://jrfibonacci.wordpress.com/2015/05/14/vanity-as-a-form-of-anxiety/
17. Iron-Deficiency Anemia. American Society of Hematology website. www.hematology.org/Patient /Anemia/Iron-Deficiency. Accessed February 29, 2020
18. Finberg KE. Unraveling mechanisms regulating systemic iron homeostasis. Hematology AM Soc Hematol Educ Program. 2011. Accessed February 29, 2020
19. Hemoglobin. MedlinePlus website. https://medlineplus.gov/ency/article//003645 November 21, 2016. Accessed February 29, 2020
20. Ferritin blood test. MedlinePlus website. https://medlineplus.gov/ency/article//003490.htm November 16, 2016, Accessed February 29, 2020

iron through the body and measures the amount of iron that is immediately available to produce RBC), attaches to it[21]. Then the iron is delivered to the liver for storage in a form, called ferritin (a protein that stores iron, so the body can use it at a later time). The RBCs, carrying the iron-rich hemoglobin, pick up fresh oxygen in the lungs and delivers it to the tissues in the body. The RBCs repeats their cycle approximately four months until they get dilapidated, the body recycles the iron to make new RBCs3.

When dealing with IDA, the body doesn't have the iron it needs for the new RBC and then the body becomes oxygen starved. If you don't have enough oxygen flowing through your body, you will be able to identify it quickly, because your lifetime of energy is rapidly depleted . But as for me, my iron and hemoglobin levels fluctuate normally .

HOW I ALMOST DIE?

It all stemmed down to neglecting ME: a lack of self-care. Two simple words that I completely abandoned. For those of you who don't know, self-care is the practice of taking action to preserve or improve one's health; also, the practice of taking an active role in protecting one's well-being and happiness, in particular during periods of stress. If you haven't done anything for yourself lately, then you need to ask yourself if you are following the second and most important commandment in the Bible, which states to "Love your neighbor as YOURSELF. There is no

---

21. Medical definition of transferrin. Medice.net website www.medicinenet.com/script/main/art march 1, 2017. Accessed February 29, 2020

commandment greater than these" (Mark 12:31). There it is, if you're not loving yourself, then how can you love your neighbor?

It all started in 2014 when my stress level increased and my menstrual cycle started getting heavier and then longer. At that time, I knew I had to watch my hemoglobin closely. I made sure to get an annual blood test to make sure my levels were normal. Things started slowing down for me and I started noticing my hemoglobin was dropping. By 2016 it dropped to a 10. This is where I should have taken action because for a female the normal level should be between 11.1 and 15.6. IDA has mild to severe symptoms, but not every patient experiences IDA symptoms. I experienced some of them, such as fatigue, mild headaches, low body temperature, tongue irritations, pica, unexpected tiredness, and weakness, just to name a few. But they were mild to moderate, so I ignored them. Nonetheless, when symptoms started showing up in the physical, like hair loss, thin fingernails, dry skin, memory loss, burning sensation, cuts on your tongue, shortness of breath, poor leg circulation, and pale skin, I knew I had to get some help.

Every year after 2016, my hemoglobin dropped one point. In 2019 my hemoglobin hit the floor and I felt it that time. I wasn't paying attention to the mild symptoms of being tired all the time. I just thought I was taking on too much responsibility at work, church, and home and needed to rest. Unfortunately, things rapidly got worse. I stopped participating in church auxiliaries and then ceased going completely. Well, there's more to that, but I'll save that for another book. I stopped shopping and only shopped for things that were necessary to survive. I put an end to helping people every time they asked. I said to myself, "Figure it out yourself." I quit reading books because I couldn't stay up. My life pretty much was at a standstill and I couldn't figure out why because my brain was so exhausted.

Then I started craving weird stuff that had a clayey texture like cake mix, flour, bread crumbs, etc. I ignored it and said I was just hungry. Then my tongue started feeling tender when I ate regular everyday food items. I disregarded it and gargled with salt water. Then my leg started feeling heavy again. I overlooked it and told myself I was getting out of shape. When I took the stairs up to my office, I realized I was only able to climb up half of the flight of stairs before I had to take a break and rest. Again, I dismissed it and said, "I need to get in the gym ASAP."

One night, my nephew woke up and said, "Something doesn't feel right. Someone is very sick." I didn't think he was talking about me, so I ignored it. There were so many other sick people that I was helping out, that I just assumed he was talking about them. Then I saw my middle sister the same night, she almost fell to the ground and said, "Death is around you." I laughed it off and went about my business slowly dragging.

My co-workers started to notice that I wasn't taking care of myself. I was so weak at that time. I wasn't getting my nails nor hair done. I was looking like "whatever at work." So they began sending encouraging messages and self-care ideas so I could start putting myself first. Other co-workers noticed that I wasn't lively anymore and wanted to know what was going on with me. I would always tell them that I just needed a nap. I had to run my space heater all day just to stay warm and my co-workers would always leave early because they would start sweating. Another one of my co-workers started offering to bring me lunch because I was too tired to walk to my car to get something to eat.

One morning I was walking to the entrance of the building and a co-worker looked at me and said, "I almost didn't speak because you are walking extremely slowly." I was walking like I was an elderly woman. It was bad. That was the eye opener for me because I started noticing how slow I was walking from the car to my desk and from my desk to the restroom. Those short distances had me huffing and puffing, but I was still going to work and trying to take care of my family. My skin started getting pale and my lips were chapped. I couldn't sleep through the night because I couldn't get enough oxygen.

After all that, I didn't ignore those symptoms. I walked to the local pharmacy (that should only take 15 minutes, but it took me 30 minutes) and purchased iron pills. I also started eating more iron-rich foods, chlorophyll drops, minerals, and vitamins. I started feeling a little better. However, I had to stop taking the iron pills because it didn't agree with my digestive system. I was back to slow dragging everywhere again, but I was still eating foods that were high-iron.

I knew from that point I needed medical help to get me through the day. I made an appointment with my OBGYN doctor and asked for stronger iron pills that won't make my stomach hurt and birth control to stop the heavy bleeding. He took one look at me and said, "You need something faster than pills." So he prescribed seven weeks of iron transfusions, to build my hemoglobin, and two rounds of Lupron shots to stop the heavy bleeding for six to nine months.

Now, here's how the evil one tried to stop my healing. After I got the prescriptions, it took the paperwork thirty days to clear. No one realized the severity of my condition because I didn't have any lab results. During those thirty days, I was getting weaker. I started to get nervous about my current state. I remember telling my sister to check on me throughout the nights because I felt like I wasn't going to make it. I recall searching the Scriptures to make sure I was good with God and making sure I forgave the people that hurt me deeply. I was preparing to die. I remembered gathering all my personal information and gave it to my mother just in case I didn't wake up.

I remember seeing my mother in the bathroom doing her hair and I walked in to talk with her. I started telling her about my personal information and she stopped in the middle of everything. She immediately laid hands on my head and started swinging me around the bathroom, praying and professing, "YOU SHALL LIVE AND NOT DIE." She wasn't playing with me that day.

On a specific day, my family was visiting. I embraced them all and went back to my room to take a nap. I was really weak that day and did not want to go to sleep. I finally snoozed off and I felt the life leave my body. I said, "No God, not like this Lord. I haven't done my work nor my calling You assigned me to do.

God, I am not ready to go. I don't have a legacy on this earth. Father, please allow me to do a great work for Your glory."

My mother invited me to her church that same weekend and I was like no, but a voice inside of me said, "Go with her." When we arrived at the church, I was miserable. All I could think of is getting back in my bed with all the lights off. Finally, we got to the last segment of the service which was communion. I was so weak I asked my sister to bring me a cup. As I ate the bread and drank the juice, I felt a spark of life flow back into me. From there I knew God heard my prayer.

Now, this is how God had it ALL under control. The Transfusion Center finally called in the midst of all that chaos and set up an appointment for me on October 9, 2019. I wanted to know what my hemoglobin number was before I started my treatments, so I was able to set up my annual blood work appointment for October 7, 2019. And two days after that, I was sitting in the chair getting treatments. So, when it seems like it's all over, please know that God is working in the background on your behalf.

Here are some scriptures you can declare while you're going through the fire.

- As for you, you meant evil against me, but God meant it for good, to bring it about that many people should be kept alive, as they are today. (Genesis 50:20 ESV)

- And we know that for those who love God all things work together for good, for those who are called according to his purpose. (Romans 8:28 ESV)
- And those whom he predestined he also called, and those whom he called he also justified, and those whom he justified he also glorified. (Romans 8:30 ESV)
- Count it all joy, my brothers, when you meet trials of various kinds, for you know that the testing of your faith produces steadfastness. And let steadfastness have its full effect, that you may be perfect and complete, lacking in nothing. (James 1:2-4 ESV)

Thank God for caring doctors that can recognize the problem and have the perfect solution. On my first visit to the infusion center, I was extremely nervous because I had never been hooked up to an IV pump and I HATED needles. So, you could imagine how I was acting in that chair. Once I was hooked up to the machine and the medicine flowed through my veins, I felt the healing process begin. When I felt like nothing could have been done, God showed me that He could work a miracle anyway He chooses.

After each dosage, something extraordinary happened.

1. October 9, 2019 – (1st Iron Infusion Treatment) Once this treatment was completed, I could breathe without thinking about it. I was able to sleep through the night. At this time, I didn't have lab work done, so I didn't know my hemoglobin level.

2. October 16, 2019 – (2nd Iron Infusion Treatment) After this treatment, it felt like oxygen ran down my legs like a rushing waterfall. From that moment, I understood and appreciated the breath of life.

3. October 17, 2019 – (Lab results - Hemoglobin) As I opened the results and my heart fell to the floor. My hemoglobin was at five. This is a dangerous level because the normal level for females should be between the numbers of 11.1 – 15.6. Doctors recommend getting a blood transfusion at an eight and here I was at a five. Everything flashed in front of my face and I understand why I was always weak and sluggish. I had most of the symptoms of IDA.

4. October 21, 2019 – (1st Lupron Treatment) This treatment was to put me into a temporary menopause stage to decrease the estrogen levels in my body and stop the heavy bleeding.

5. October 23, 2019 – (3rd Iron Infusion Treatment) I felt great and full of energy. I was able to walk up the stairs at work and even go out to lunch with coworkers. I was feeling alive again.

6. October 28, 2019 – (Lab results – Iron Treatments) I received the results of the three treatments and it was at a 6.7. I was shocked because I felt so much better and was able to dance again. But I guess when your hemoglobin is super low, any number above it will make you feel alive.

7. My nurse called the next day and said, "How are you still going to work and walking around?" All I could say was, "God did it." He still has work for me to do on this earth. She told me to sit down most of the day at work to preserve energy.

8. October 30, 2019 – (1st HOT FLASH). My God!! Let me pause right here so I can say a prayer for the women that are going through menopause. FATHER GOD in the name of the Almighty JESUS, please send us cool fresh wind from on high. Amen. Hot flashes are real!

9. November 6, 2019 – (4th Iron Infusion Treatment) After this treatment, I felt better and went shopping again, but I found out I was only at a 7.6. I was still in the weak zone, but feeling much better.

10. November 7, 2019 – (5th Iron Infusion treatment) I was feeling stronger after this treatment and was able to go shopping yet again. However, I was only at a 9, which is still low.

11. January 13, 2019 – (2nd Lupron Treatment) Before I received this treatment, I called in for prayer and started taking vitamin E capsules. The flashes were not as frequent and didn't last as long. Things were getting better.

12. January 31, 2020 – (6th Iron Infusion Treatment) I felt so energetic because my Hemoglobin reached an awesome level of 12.9.

13. February 7, 2020 – (7th Iron Infusion Treatment) The 7th treatment, on the 7th day, the number of completion. Oh yes! I am going somewhere with this. We know that the number seven is represented in the Bible as the completion and perfection of things that are both physical and spiritual. God Himself introduced this number to mark the completion of His work of Creation. I felt like a whole person again. I felt like God was saying to me personally to take up my bed, walk, and be made whole.

After the last treatment, all I heard in my spirit was the Scripture that states "The glory of the latter temple should be greater than the former says the Lord of hosts. And in this place, I will give peace, says the Lord of hosts (Haggai 2:9)." This life changing experience transformed my whole life. I have even more energy to accomplish the calling on my life.

This experience made me a stronger person in the Word of God and enjoying life more as I take out time to give myself SELF-CARE. Remember to take time out for YOU!!!! Love on YOU!!! YOU are worth it!!!!!!

WARNING SIGNS/RED FLAGS

When real life suddenly begins, many people need to be cognizant not to neglect the self-care regimen. Neglecting yourself while helping others is a dangerous place to be in. Conversely, in some situations, it is unavoidable. Being aware of the warning signs/red flags, the body is trying to communicate to us is key. A great deal of time, we wait to see the message on the billboards saying, "Warning-warning something is wrong." However, we know that life doesn't work in that manner. When it comes to the body, being tuned in is critical. Ignoring life's warning signs will create complications and, in some cases, danger with serious consequences. 1 Corinthians 6:19-20 states, what? Know ye not that your body is the temple of the Holy Ghost [which is] in you, which ye have of God, and ye are not your own? For ye are bought with a price: therefore glorify God in your body, and in your spirit, which are God's. Therefore, be a good steward over your body.

Listed below were some of the warning signs/red flags I've experienced.

- Unexpected tiredness/Fatigue – When you are getting 8 -10 hours of sleep per night and performing simple activities becomes harsh and tasks to the body.
- Poor brain function – When you are having memory loss and difficulty concentrating on simple tasks.
- Shortness of breath- When you stop to think about catching your breath.
- Cold hands and feet – When you cannot stay warm throughout the day and need a space heater to keep warm.
- Pale skin – When your skin starts to abnormally lighten.
- Burning sensation in the tongue – When the tongue has abnormal cuts and is sensitive to acidic foods.

- Pica – When you are craving unhealthy items such as ice, clay, dirt, chalk, paint, etc.
- Poor leg circulation – When your legs feel heavier than usual.
- Hair & nails – When your hair starts to fall out suddenly and your nails become thinner.
- Other warning signs/red flags may include:
- Weakness
- Dizziness
- Headaches
- Low body temperature
- Hypothyroidism
- Adrenal fatigue
- Spoon-shaped finger and toenails
- Smooth tongue
- Sores at the corners of the mouth
- Dry skin
- Ringing in the ears (tinnitus)
- Leg pains
- Chest pain
- Heartburn

If you have experienced any of these symptoms, please contact your doctor.

LESSONS LEARNED

When you have symptoms of IDA, or any disease, DON'T IGNORE it! You should always pray about it and ask for God's guidance on the right doctor for your needs.

It would be best to request a yearly physical exam (no matter the cost) with basic blood work. The Basic Health Panel (BHP) is imperative to request each year to monitor your overall health. This will benefit you as well as your doctors to understand what steps to take to improve your health if needed. For example, if your lab results show high or low levels in a particular area, your healthcare providers can immediately recommend a lifestyle change and/or, habits or prescribe early treatment to reduce the risk of developing diseases.

Listed below are examples of basic labs you may want to request from your doctors each year.

- Basic Chemistry testing, LIPIDS and Complete Blood Count
- Thyroid, 4-Panel: T4, T3, TSH, & the Free Thyroxine Index (Thyroid) - The thyroid gland primarily regulates the body's metabolism.
- Hemoglobin A 1 C - A test used to assess glucose levels over the last 2-3 months for people with diabetes.
- Vitamin D, 25-Hydroxy: Vitamin D plays a key role in maintaining several aspects of overall health.

Once you receive your results, don't be fearful of asking your doctor to explain everything that you do not understand in great details. Moreover, extensive research on the specific symptoms would give you the advantage to learn more about how to eliminate or manage before it gets out of control.

Listen to the people around you who love you. This can be a lifesaver. They can see subtle or dramatic changes in your lifestyle and give you advice to seek help.

Practicing daily self-care is vital. Everyone needs to take time out to learn about themselves and what they need to live each day. Sometimes you can be too busy to pay attention to the symptoms. Make sure you take time out to understand the new you in every new season!

CHAPTER 10

Birth

BY JALONZO SAMUELS

Death was after me prior to my birth. My biological mother was fourteen years old when she got pregnant with me and because of a medical condition she had and her age, the doctors informed her that if she continued with the pregnancy, she would lose her life. She now had a major decision to make continue with her pregnancy and die or abort me and so she could live. Can you imagine being fourteen years old with a full life in front of you, dreams and aspirations to fulfill to be faced with this dilemma? She was still a child. Everyone was telling her to abort me and live, that her life could continue to flourish without the burden of attempting to do both. She had a tough decision to make, because whatever she decided there would be death to either for her or me. Well, at fourteen years old, she made that decision. She told the doctors, "Let him live, even if it takes my life."

On December 11, 1955, at 1:42 a.m., my biological mother gave birth to me. She died eight minutes after my birth. At that moment, I became motherless. The hospital placed me in the orphan care unit. My now-deceased mother's family did not want me, for they felt that I was the cause of her death and to the most part, I was, but God had a BIGGER plan. There was a husband and wife that had been trying to conceive for years. You see, the wife found out after many years of trying that she had a rare condition, the same as my mother, that would not allow her to conceive, so they were looking to adopt a child. Now watch God... They happened to be at the very same hospital visiting a friend of theirs and from what I was told, they decided to visit the children's ward and spoke to a nurse about adopting a child. This nurse walked them to the nursery, and they saw me. They asked about my story and once they heard it, they began the process to make me their own. Well, three weeks later, I had a mother and a father. They were both professional people, a school teacher, and a business owner. I now had a family that loved me, that gave me their name and all that they had I now had.

Ephesians 1:5 states that Father God had adopted us and predestinated us unto Himself according to the good pleasure of His Will to the Praise of His Glory before the foundation of the world. The enemy placed a death sentence on us all, but through the finished work of the Cross, He gave us life. Though death had been pronounced upon me in my biological mother's womb, God had already created a vessel and a circumstance in my adopted parents' lives that death would not overtake me, but life would be for me so that His Glory would shine forth in and through my life.

WARNING SIGNS

My biological mother was considered a high-risk pregnancy.

LESSONS LEARNED

Through the process of my birth and the opportunity for death, even before life could begin for me, I have come to realize and know that the Father's Plan for me did not end at the thoughts or wishes of those that only perceived life in a carnal sense. Life is totally determined, spiritually, through God's Plan and not by the helm of those who do not understand the Sovereignty of God's Mind.

***

POSSIBLE DEATH IN THE WOMB

BY TRÉASA BROWN

My testimony of how I was conceived, is a unique testimony to tell because my mother prayed for me and wrote my name on a Christmas stocking before I was even born a year in advance, (the year of 1987 to be exact). That's faith! It would be much harder for my mother to conceive due to her tubes being tied and the doctors reversing them. They told her the chances of her getting pregnant would be very low. Thinking upon mother's prayer, I'm often reminded of Hannah, when she, in bitterness of the soul, made her petition unto the Lord that if He gave her a man child, she would give him, (Samuel) back to the Lord all the days of his life (See I Samuel 1:9-11).

My mother just happened to pray for a girl! I also have been a child that was dedicated back to God. Hannah's prayer, as we know, it was answered!

I Samuel 1:27 says, "For this child I prayed: and the Lord hath given me my petition which I asked of him."

The Lord made that conception possible and as He did for my mother. Her pregnancy was very complicated due to me trying to arrive early at the third month of pregnancy. She was contracting and many of us know that contractions are a stage of ACTIVE labor and takes place when the baby is READY to be birthed. Anyone that knows about pregnancy also knows that the chances of a baby's survival at three months are very slim. The baby is very underdeveloped and at the beginning stages of development. There are still many stages of crucial growth for the baby. The third month is considered the last month of the 1st trimester. The complications caused my mother to be on bed rest for most of her pregnancy. She was spotting, and had to wear a Tokos belt, which monitors contractions. If she had more than ten contractions within a certain amount of time, she was to go to the ER to be hooked to an IV. She also experienced intense morning sickness, along with pain.

I have heard before, that Prophets or Prophetic people seem to have detrimental experiences at young ages or even later on in life. The enemy desires to take them out! All I can say is, this is a mark of letting you know that you are destined for greatness and the enemy wants to stop what God has already predestined, but he can't! The blood of Jesus still works and still covers! When you have an anointing upon your life, there's a mandate and assignment that must be carried out! Your anointing brings on warfare! When I say that I'm a walking, talking miracle, I'm just that! I also was a meconium stained baby. Meconium stain is defined as the dark green substance forming the first feces of a newborn infant. If inhaled by the baby, it can lead to respiratory issues. This caused my mother to have an emergency C-section. I shouldn't be here right now, but the Lord saw to it to keep me here! I could've died a premature death while in my mother's womb. But I made it! Just think of how precious the little ones are in the sight of God! In America, we see so many abortions and the shedding of innocent blood, which is one of the very things that the Lord hates and is an abomination unto Him. The Bible declares in Proverbs 6:16-17, "These six things doth the Lord hate: yea seven are an abomination unto him: A proud look, a lying tongue, and hands that shed innocent blood."

We must ask ourselves, why do we see so much of this in our country? Why doesn't a woman think twice before killing what the Lord God Almighty has placed in her womb? It is stated according to abortion statistics, that from January to March of 2019, there have been 208,000 abortions and counting.[22] These

---

22. Heffernan, Katie. "Abortion Statistics," Springfield Right to Life, March 26, 2019. Accessed February 15, 2020, https://www.springfieldrtl.org/abortion-statistics/

statistics are mind blowing! Do you not know that you are carrying greatness on the inside of you? We are made in the image and likeness of God according to Genesis 1:27 which declares, "So God created man in HIS OWN image, in the image of God created he him; male and female created he them." Many need to reconsider! You are killing one with destiny, purpose, and that could leave an impact for the Kingdom of God!

The Bible also declares in Psalm 139:13-14, "For thou hath possessed my reins: thou hast covered me in my mother's womb. I will praise thee; for I am fearfully and wonderfully made: marvelous are thy works; and that my soul knoweth right well."

So many women in this world don't consider what they are carrying on the inside of them. They don't think about their child's destiny and who the Lord is calling and forming them to be. We have become a selfish nation, only concerned about ourselves, rather than what grieves God! We don't count up the cost of our decisions and we'd rather kill off life than watch it grow and see what it will become. As it is in the natural, we see this in the spirit. Don't let what you are carrying on the inside of your spiritual womb die on the inside of you! God meant for purpose to be BIRTHED out. He wants us to bring forth much fruit and produce with what lies dormant on the inside of us. Had my mother lost me, look what would've been gone. A prophetic voice, a Prophetess, one who was destined for greatness in Christ Jesus, would've been missing! I say this humbly.

I remember dreading to turn thirty because the enemy had caused me to think that something was going to happen to me at that age. I remember telling people, "It will be a blessing if I even make it to thirty." For years, while in my 20's, I feared that age because of what the devil planted in my mind. But the Lord had a purpose for me to be here! I was purposed to live and not die.

Psalms 118:17-18 declares, "I shall not die, but live, and declare the works of the Lord. The Lord hath chastened me sore: but he hath not given me over unto death."

The enemy has been after my life since my mother's womb, so it's evident that there's not only purpose in me, but there's destiny to be birthed and brought forth out of me. All for the glory and honor of God. We don't want to be an aid in helping the enemy to kill the destinies of others, but we want to build the Kingdom of God!

In John 10:10, Jesus declares, The THIEF cometh not, but for to STEAL, and to KILL, and to DESTROY: I am come that they might have LIFE, and that they might have it more ABUNDANTLY.

Not only could I have been taken out in the womb, but the enemy has threatened to take my life verbally and tried to come through dreams. There was a time that I was in my sister's room and late at night, I heard a voice say, "I'm going to take your life." It startled me, but I began to speak back to that voice and rebuked what was said to me.

In my dream, I was in a hallway and as I stood there, a woman passed by and told me the exact date of my death. She had no emotion when she spoke and continued down the hallway like nothing was wrong. I remember feeling so sad that I knew I had to tell my family about my death. As I proceeded to tell my mother, she grabbed my hand and pulled out a needle, and I believe she stuck me with it. It was the type of needle that doctors use when they are ready to administer an injection. From my hand, I saw in detail, where a blood drop fell onto the ground. That's all I remember from the dream.

I was told in prayer not to receive this dream because the adversary sent it. What am I saying? The enemy wants to kill your destiny, so he tries to kill you in the process! He will try to kill off what's in your womb, not just naturally, but spiritually. There is VALUE in what you are carrying! To the women that are contemplating getting an abortion or those that have supported it. STOP! Reconsider what you are doing and what you're aiding! You are supporting murder and have become a murderer.

The Bible declares in John 8:44, "Ye are of your father the devil, and the lusts of your father ye will do. He was a murderer from the beginning, and abode not in the truth, because there is no truth in him. When he speaketh a lie, he speaketh of his own: for he is a liar, and the father of it."

Repent! The Lord is faithful and just to forgive. Ask the Lord to regulate your mind! If I may be transparent right here, the enemy presented an opportunity to get rid of my youngest son.

I had already had two children out of wedlock and my third one was on the way. I was told to get rid of my child, but I ignored the vessel that the enemy was speaking through. I choose to take on the challenge and to persevere, as I didn't want the shedding of innocent blood on my hands! It's dangerous to override the Bible and to fall into the hands of an angry God! The Lord brought me out alright, despite my situation in being a single mother of three. I love my children and now understand that the Lord has a plan for their lives, just as He does for mine. They are a gift from God regardless of my circumstances!

People dwell on their careers, current situations, and future to make those things an excuse to have an abortion. This is coming from a selfish and immature place. We need the Lord to help us and deliver us from all evil. Many may argue that when the baby is just a fetus, they aren't alive until a certain stage of development. But the devil is a liar! Anything that the Lord takes time to form and create already exists. It already IS. Our God is a LIVING God! Be careful who you are being influenced by and who's telling you to kill off what God wants to exist. You're not just taking lives, but you're killing off destinies. Don't kill what's in your womb!

WARNING SIGNS

1. Early Contractions

My mother's contractions began early with pain.

2. Spotting

My mother experienced some spotting along the way.

3. Tokos Belt

This was a monitor belt that was worn around my mother's belly to count the contractions per hour that she was having. If she had ten contractions within a certain amount of time, then she would have to go to the emergency room to be hooked to an IV, which took about an hour to administer.

4. Sickness

My mother couldn't really eat anything because of the intense morning sickness. She had a sensitivity to certain smells, especially cooked meat.

LESSONS LEARNED
1. The enemy comes to steal, kill, and destroy! The devil not only wants to kill you but your destiny.
2. Don't let the enemy physically and spiritually kill what's on the inside of you!.
3. Speak to the enemy when he tries to pronounce death over you! Declare and decree LIFE.
4. Prophets and Prophetic voices are a threat to the kingdom of darkness.
5. God chose you prophet/prophetess and you are destined for greatness.

CHAPTER 11

Blood Clots

BY MICHELLE LOATMAN

Since I was about 10 years old, I have had issues with my legs. My calves were significantly larger than my peers. The kids would often make fun of me, and I was self-conscious of their size. I would do everything in my power to refrain from wearing shorts, dresses or skirts. People would laugh at me and call me "cankles" "tree trunks," etc. I also had enlarged veins that were visibly appalling to the eye. My mom and my great aunt had this same problem. As I got older and increasingly obese, my veins became damaged and began to bulge profusely throughout my legs.

Unfortunately, at the age of 17, I also picked up the habit of smoking. After years of smoking, lack of living a healthy lifestyle and being overweight, then having two children back-to-back, put more strain on the health of my legs. In my early twenties, I already had the varicose veins of an 80-year-old woman. I was under the direct care of a heart doctor, who gave me compression stockings to relieve some of the pressure. This only worked, seldomly, especially since I hadn't made any dietary lifestyle changes. The blood that flowed through my legs, that was supposed to go down to my feet, and pump back up to my heart and brain began collecting in my legs. The doctor explained to me that we have flaps in the middle of our legs. These flaps are like doorways. They were created to open to let some blood in and then close the door back until it was time for that blood to cycle back up to the top. This process also contributes to the generation of oxygen throughout our body as well.

At the age of 25 and having had an ultrasound of the blood flow in my legs not working properly, my doctor scheduled me for surgery. I had a procedure called, Endovenous Ablation of Varicose Veins, also known as vein closure done. "Endovenous ablation uses energy to cauterize (burn) and close varicose veins. Doctors use it to help ease symptoms such as pain, swelling, and irritation." [23]After my outpatient procedure, my legs were dressed in bandages, and I was sent home on bed rest for a day. Instructions were given to prop my legs above the heart level whenever pain or swelling would occur. My body seemed to adjust to the procedure, for the most part. However, because I had no changes in my diet and exercise regimen, and I was standing

---

23. Radiology Society of North America (RSNA) (2020). Varicose Vein Treatment (Endovenous Ablation of Varicose Veins). February 15, 2020. Retrieved from: https://www.radiologyinfo.org/en/info.cfm?pg=varicoseabl

on my feet to work 12 hours for one job, two part-time jobs and going to school, I was not giving my legs proper rest time.

I decided to go on a diet. I would go with a couple of colleagues of mine to a doctor . in Chester, Pennsylvania, and he would give us a B-12, some other shot, and Phen Phen pills to last a couple of weeks. My appetite decreased tremendously. I would often get full after 1-2 bites of cereal in the morning. I would drink water all day, take water pills to take off water weight from my body, preferably my legs, and I increased my exercise. I would workout or go for walks with my colleagues on my lunch break, and then turn around and workout again at night. I even started doing belly dancing. I went from 235 lbs. to 165 lbs. in a matter of months. While my legs decreased, they were still big. Sometimes I would wear my compression stockings. But I wasn't elevating my legs at night or staying off my feet more. Even when I was home I was running around cleaning, doing stuff for the kids, and doing things for others. I never rested. When someone had an emergency, I would make it my emergency.

At the age of 33, I had my own emergency. Over the years, I had gained a few pounds back. I began stress eating and was still smoking. My legs started getting worse. At this point, the doctor decided that vein stripping would be best. "Varicose vein stripping is a surgical procedure that removes varicose veins from the legs or thighs." [24]The procedure is an outpatient surgery, just like the vein closure. They never told me that if you

---

24. Johnson, Shannon. January 5, 2016. Your Look Your Way. Varicose Vein Stripping. Healthline. February 15, 2020. Retrieved from: https://www.healthline.com/health/varicose-vein-stripping

have ever had a major illness in the area where the veins are to be extracted , you may not have that option available. My mom had had this procedure done years prior, so I didn't see any risk factors for me. Except for the one I forgot; she didn't smoke. The procedure went well, and I was back home by the end of the day on bed rest. I scheduled the procedure purposely on a Friday because I knew my job would be calling my phone for questions and issues they wanted me to address. I had planned on resting for a day and going out the next day to pick up a few things for my children's father's birthday. That never happened.

As the day went on, I got up to use the bathroom and even smoke, although strictly prohibited by the doctor's instructions. I figured I had smoked before after the last procedure and after getting my wisdom teeth extracted. The doctors warned me not to do it then. But hey, I'm still here aren't I? By mid-afternoon, I began to have some discomfort in my legs. For the most part, I felt the bruising and cuts from the procedure. But something just didn't feel right. By dinner time, I had excruciating pain behind my right knee and I was getting scared. I propped my legs up on the pillows and just figured the pain was coming from the uncomfortable way the bandages were rolling up at the knee pit of my legs. I figured I would sleep it off and be fine by the morning. However, I went to get up to use the bathroom and my legs almost gave out on me. Unlike when I came home from the procedure, I didn't have the strength to walk as well. Again, due to my leg's health track record, I figured it was due to laying down with my legs wrapped for too long. But the pain kept getting worse. I called my sister, and she strongly suggested I go to the hospital to get checked out. She came to pick me up and we went to the ER. The place was jammed packed with patients waiting to be seen for various emergencies.

I figured once I told the intake nurse my emergency, they would get me in and out in no time. I planned to be back home playing with my boys by morning. Wrong again! I sat, sat and sat some more in the waiting room area. After several hours of waiting, I was called back and taken into a room for an ultrasound. Then I was taken down to get a CAT scan done. By the time I was finished with that, I was limping and walking like a tortoise. I felt like my legs were going to give out at any moment. I was put in another room filled with beds of people. Left for another interim of waiting.

Sometime before midnight, the doctor came into the room and said the words I dreaded the most. "Ms. Loatman, you are not supposed to be here! If you had laid down and went to sleep, you would have been dead before morning. You have a Deep Vein Thrombosis (DVT) in your leg that has spread up to each chamber of your lungs, causing four massive, life-threatening Pulmonary Embolisms (PEs). Over 350,000 people are affected by Deep Vein Thrombosis and Pulmonary Embolisms a year. "On average, one person dies every six minutes from a blood clot." [25]Diagnoses are often overlooked and the diagnosis, in most cases, is not found until after death. DVT & PEs are significant with the elderly, bedridden patients in long term facilities, people who have had prior diagnoses, sitting for long periods of time in a chair, and traveling for long periods of time.

---

25. National Blood Clot Alliance. Stop the Clot. Signs and Symptoms. February 15, 2020. Retrieved from: https://www.stoptheclot.org/blood-clot-information/blood-clots-in-the-united-states/

Most people, no matter what age, are never diagnosed with these kinds of health conditions. In this set of circumstances, we are delivering the news to family members who are getting ready to head down a journey of planning their loved one's funeral. I don't understand how this is possible. You have quite a journey ahead of you young lady."

That night I was wheeled to a room where I would spend the next eight days in recovery. It was one of the scariest times in my life. For the first time, I wasn't able to do anything. I couldn't walk. I couldn't bath myself. I was dependent on others to care for me. This was the worst feeling for me because all of my memories of relying on the people I should have been able to trust never worked out for me. I felt I was an insignificant burden on others for so long that I took matters into my own hands since I was a teen. I didn't want to rely on anyone. But I realized, the one I had to rely on most was God. I had to stop doing things my way. My way was going to get me killed. God's grace and mercy had saved me from so much before. But I took it for granted. I had been saved since I was 17, but I was still doing things my way. I was taking risks with my spiritual and physical life, never thinking of the consequences. My best friend and my sister came to the hospital and helped me with getting out of the bed, washing up and making sure I was resting. Oh yeah, because I forgot to mention, I was in my hospital bed completing my finals for one of my classes and doing paperwork that my job had sent for me to complete in order to remain on the payroll , even though I was on salary.

I remember being in so much pain and hooked up to heart monitors. I was unable and unwilling to take certain pain medications because of the side effects. One day the doctors came in and said they were going to give me morphine in my IV. I had never had that before and thought that was something you give people who are dying from cancer or some other life-threatening illness. I remember my mom came to visit me and she was sitting in the chair in the corner, facing me. When they gave me the morphine, I had an encounter like never before. It felt like I was dying. It literally felt like a hand had reached into my chest cavity, grabbed a hold of my heart until it stopped beating, and I drifted off to sleep. I remember my mom telling me how mortified she was when she saw my facial expression. She said my entire face distorted like it was another person inside of me. We were both afraid.

I was on different blood thinners while in the hospital and learning how to eat in accordance with the medication. When you are taking blood thinners, you must be careful not to eat certain foods that would interact with your medicine and cause your blood to thin out so much that you would have internal bleeding. Once I left the hospital, I had to go to the lab every other day to check my blood levels, to ensure the blood wasn't too thin, and not too thick to the point of clotting. I couldn't eat whatever I wanted without checking the contents. I had to wear an alert bracelet with my medical information, in the event of an accident. Also, at the time of my blood clots, I was taking birth control, Nuvaring. It was an internal, rubber-like ring that I had been on for 11 years. So not only was I not supposed to be smoking with the surgery, I was aware, but took for granted, that you are prohibited from smoking while on birth control. I was out of work for 2 months, although I did the paperwork and other tasks for work at home. I walked with a cane and had to physically regain my strength and ability to walk to full capacity.

"But as for you, you meant evil against me; but God meant it for good, in order to bring it about as it is this day, to save many people alive." (Genesis 50:20)

I feel truly blessed by God's mercy and grace for living through this situation, as He has delivered me from numerous situations. Not only did God bring me out alive, and restored health back unto me, but he also blessed me with my little girl. Just six months after being diagnosed with the blood clots and being told that I would not be able to have any more children because my body had been through too much. On Christmas morning of this year, I found out I was pregnant.

WARNING SIGNS

Deep vein thrombosis (DVT) occurs when a blood clot forms in one of the deep veins of your body, usually in your legs, but sometimes in your arm. The signs and symptoms of a DVT include:

- Swelling, usually in one leg (or arm)
- Leg pain or tenderness often described as a cramp or Charley horse
- Reddish or bluish skin discoloration
- Leg (or arm) warm to touch

These symptoms of a blood clot may feel like a pulled muscle or a "Charley horse," but may differ in that the leg (or arm) may be swollen, slightly discolored, and warm." (NBCA) You could see from the side of my right calf, all the way up my leg, a red wine color.

"Clots can break off from a DVT and travel to the lung, causing a pulmonary embolism (PE), which can be fatal." The signs and symptoms of a PE include:

- Sudden shortness of breath
- Chest pain-sharp, stabbing; may get worse with a deep breath
- Rapid heart rate
- Unexplained cough, sometimes with bloody mucus (NBCA)

While these are generally the symptoms, I was not having shortness of breath or pain in my chest. The one sign that I had, that I would always override, up until a couple of years ago, was my gut instinct. That guide on the inside. The Holy Spirit will speak to us when something is not right, or when God is leading us to go somewhere, say something, etc. If you continue to ignore it, you will desensitize yourself from it. I have also experienced, now that my walk with the Lord is closer, that the feeling gets so strong sometimes, that I can't breathe, or I feel nausea until I heed the warning.

LESSONS LEARNED

The enemy has tried to take me out of here before my time, many times throughout my life. But, in this instance, I was assisting him. I was giving him a foothold. I was slowly killing myself and living out of the will of God, despite declaring I was saved. I knew some of the words. I went to church. I learned that I was essentially committing suicide, which is a sin. All death is not instant, and all death is not physical.

"Do you not know that you are the temple of God and that the Spirit of God dwells in you? (1 Corinthians 3:16 NKJV)

I learned that giving into the lust of your flesh can and will kill you. While it was determined that the bandages on my legs were tied too tightly, I am adamant that if I was not smoking right after surgery, in combination with smoking with the birth control, and if I was not living a life of carnality while proclaiming to be a Christian, that I could have avoided the blood clots. I was vexing the Holy Spirit in many ways. It was only by God's grace and mercy, His calling, and purpose on my life that has allowed me to still be here on this earth today. God is a faithful God to keep His Word, and I am truly thankful.

CHAPTER 12

Brain Aneurysm

BY ALLENA DOUGLAS

I worked as a registered nurse with two jobs. I was enrolled in many certification classes, working overtime to enhance and propel my career. At this time in my life, I started to party and hang out. My prayer life and church attendance suffered. Of course, to deal with my guilt, I would occasionally attend church and slip in. I became popular by hosting parties, going out with friends and coworkers. I thought I was living the life. I enjoyed being with everyone and the notoriety. Despite the fun and attention, I still felt empty.

I remember working hard daily. I would tell my coworkers I was having headaches. I didn't pay attention to this because I had been a migraine sufferer since age 12. I didn't suffer from hypertension and I worked out 3-4 times a week.

On March 3, 2010, I was working on the ward with my two military techs. We were working very hard. Dan and Nick told me they had a mandatory layout the next day. I told them to do their layout and I would finish up all the groups, notes, and my nursing duties as well. The last thing I remember from that night was an angry, defiant patient on my caseload.

I suffered a subarachnoid brain aneurysm rupture. I give credit to the quick action of my staff who attended to me and notified the house Supervisor, Colonel Lue Reeves. After performing hands-on CPR, I was transported to our hospital's ER, where I was quickly stabilized and transported to Candler/St Joseph's hospital in Savannah, Georgia. I remember waking up on the operating table. I heard Dr. Howington yelling at the staff because there was a defect with a crucial piece of equipment needed to perform the surgery. Dr. Howington said, "Every minute counts. She can die or be a vegetable." Before I could be afraid, the Holy Spirit said, I will never leave you nor forsake you. Fear not neither be dismayed." (Abbreviated, Deuteronomy 31:8)

I was subsequently transferred to Memorial Health University Hospital in Savannah, Georgia and the surgery was performed two days later.

My family came quickly and they were told to expect the worst. They were told that I would most likely suffer major neurological deficits or even death. The odds were not good. According to the Brain Aneurysm Foundation, the survival rates are 1 to 3 where aneurysmal subarachnoid aneurysm survivors recover without any disabilities. 0-40% die within the first 30 days.[26]

My family met with my neurosurgeon, Dr. Jay Howington. He decided to do a more dangerous procedure, a craniotomy, because it would give me a better quality of life with better outcomes of survival. I thank God for giving me one of the top surgeons in the world.

Hours after my surgery, I began to text and call people on my telephone. These were miraculous signs so early after such an extensive brain surgery. Dr. Howington was in disbelief that I was writing full sentences and doing well so soon after surgery. Dr. Howington brought interns to my room to meet me. He told them, "I don't know what your beliefs are, but her recovery is a miracle from God."

I remember the flood of people at my bedside. The overwhelming support, prayers, and gifts were heartwarming. I was discharged from the hospital two weeks later. I walked out of the hospital. I didn't require physical therapy, speech therapy, or occupational therapy. What a blessing. My initial recovery was rough because I experienced fatigue and headaches. I began my quest to get in the right relationship with God. I prayed and read my Bible daily.

---

26. Brain Aneurysm Foundation. https://bafound.org

I remembered the beautiful visions of what I believed to be heaven. I saw the most beautiful large buildings, streams, the greenest grass and trees. There was a very bright light and an overwhelming feeling of peace. I wanted to go there but couldn't. The Holy Spirit spoke and said, "There is more for you to do."

I returned to work in three months because I was told that my condition wasn't covered by workman's compensation. I didn't know that I could have appealed that decision. I had to combat the fatigue and memory deficits. I dealt with a boss that didn't care about my recovery and made it difficult for me. She was later reported and removed from that position. I was moved to a position with a promotion and a fixed schedule.

As I approach each day with gratitude, I see that life is a gift. Some people who aren't in Christ can't understand my passion. God allowed me to live. I have yet another day with my children and grandchildren, who are my motivation. Their love, support, and encouragement have opened my eyes even further to appreciate the beautiful gift of life. I have been asked, "Why do you work so hard? Why do you do all of that?" I really believe my work is ordained by God. And Whatsoever you do, do it heartily as to the Lord, and not unto men. ▫Colossians 3:23

I work very hard to give back through service by providing the very best care for my patients and working to educate my community about brain aneurysms. I have a yearly follow-up to ensure that my aneurysm is stable. I have had a few setbacks, but I am back on track and committed to staying healthy and educating others. Yearly, I engage my legislature about making September National Brain Aneurysm Month.

I will continue my journey to educate, inform, and advocate the importance of awareness of this devastating cause. I've met many people through The Brain Aneurysm Foundation. Each one has their own story of: survival, appreciation for what we still have, loss and triumph, gratitude and grief. We all share an appreciation for being, having survived, and empowering others to make it through.

I almost died. I am a recipient of God's divine miraculous healing. I will continually have a praise of thanksgiving in my heart and will be heard from my mouth. My faith has been restored. I am humbled to be a recipient of God's grace and mercy. In everything I do, God will be glorified.

WARNING SIGNS

I had an increase in headaches and they felt different than usual. They usually affected my frontal region, but these were in the occipital area.

LESSON LEARNED

- God is faithful despite our faults.
- I am honored that I am a recipient of God's miraculous healing power.

CHAPTER 13

Car Accident

BY JALONZO SAMUELS

I had just gotten married to my wife, Yolanda, on October 13, 2018. We went on our personal envoy for seven days, came back, and began to start our lives together. October 22, 2018 was a beautiful morning. All was blissful and I dropped my wife off to work. I have not secured employment as of yet, because I moved to my wife's hometown where she was working in the school district and had her own business there. So, I didn't think that it would be fair to make her move to my city, so I came to her. After I dropped my wife off, I figured that I would handle some immediate business in another city. I was driving, enjoying the day, listening to the radio, just taking my time, and had not a care in the world. I went to the attorney's office only to find out that he would not be in that day. I should have called and followed my first mind. Well, on my way back, I decided to stop at a convenience store to get a soda pop.

As I began to turn into the store, let me say this first, I looked both ways and nothing was coming, but when I turned, out of nowhere, BOOM... A car T-boned me, traveling at 60 miles per hour. I was knocked unconscious. I was told that they had to pull me out of the car because it was believed that it would catch on fire. When I came back to reality, I was in the back of the E.M.T vehicle with IV's, etc. Here, again, was the enemy trying to take my life, but the Lord said NO... In Psalm 91, we are assured that we that dwell in the secret place shall abide in the shadow of the Almighty. That God is our refuge and that He shall deliver us from the snare of the fowler. He will give His angels charge over us to keep us in all our ways and that we shall be satisfied with long life. His salvation shall belong to us. I am thankful for His Secret Place.

WARNING SIGNS

There were no warning signs as I traveled to my destination on that day. There were no unctions in my spirit that told me not to go. It was a matter that needed to be dealt with and I had the time to go, so I did.

WHAT I LEARNED

Though there were no warning signs about the accident, I did come to learn two great truths concerning the accident. I did not inform my wife of my plans to go that morning and by not doing so, it almost destroyed her sanity when she found out about the severity of the crash. Secondly, I came to be thankful to and for Father's Sovereignty over my life, that just as death could not hold Jesus down, He was the plan and purpose of God, death did not have victory over me, for His plan and purpose for my life would stand as well.

SUMMARY

Warning always comes before destruction and I know that my disobedience was the thing that could have brought death to me. Yet I would ask myself at times that after all these brushings with death, why was death always lurking at my door? Why would death come after me at birth, at fourteen, at twenty-eight, and even now? Did my parents or I do something to merit an early death? My answer came to me in the John 9:3, all these things happened so that the Work and Glory of God should be made manifest... I am just so thankful for His Amazing Grace!

I am here today to tell you that I have learned through all these ordeals that The Word of God is TRUTH and that God Alone Is Sovereign. Death could not take Jesus until His time and purpose were fulfilled on the earth AND THIS IS TRUE FOR YOU AND FOR ME.

***

CAR ACCIDENT

BY KIMBERLY MOSES

I got a temporary license permit when I was fourteen. I was so excited and often begged my parents to use their car. Sometimes they would let me drive to the store across the street when it would benefit them. A year later, I grew tired of not having my own vehicle. I knew my parents were going through some financial hardships, so I was determined to work hard to purchase my own transportation. I was good at braiding because I stayed in the mirror for hours of corn rolling designs in my hair. People would stop me in the hallway at school to ask who did my hair. The word spread and my schedule was packed. After school and on the weekends, I would braid hair. Even some of my teachers came to my parents' house to get serviced.

Money started to add up and I was able to buy my car with cash around my 16th birthday. However, I aspired to become an exotic dancer and discontentment set in my heart about braiding hair. All I wanted to do was party at the club, but my busy schedule didn't allow me to go as much. Everyone thought that I would become a cosmetologist. But on my 18th birthday, I went to the strip club and got a job.

I was heading down a dark path. I constantly looked over my shoulders because the women hated me. They saw me as a threat. I remember my first night of dancing. I made a few hundred dollars. When I finished, all the women in the dressing room ganged up on me and the one in charge cursed me out.

She accused me of stealing her client. I didn't see their point of view because I felt it was a fair game. I was the better hustler, younger and prettier. I knew she was jealous. I endured that harsh environment for a few weeks before heading to another club.

One day, I met a man on the internet, and we started dating. He was about 20 years older than me, jealous and possessive. I was his trophy. We lived together for about six months and he wanted to marry me. He introduced me to his mother. She was a devoted Christian. At this point, I never was around churchgoers and I knew she was different. I could sense that she was holy, and God's hand was upon her life. My ex-boyfriend and his mother took me to church. Never have I felt so uncomfortable. I knew that I was a sinner when I walked into the building. I felt dirty and ashamed of my lifestyle. I fought tears the whole service and wanted to run outside. I didn't realize that the Lord was working on me.

A few weeks went by and my ex-boyfriend started to listen to Fred Hammond. He had just released a new album. He would blast his CD in the car as we traveled from California to New Mexico then to Texas. Through this album, seeds of the gospel were planted in my heart. I started becoming more aware of my sinful lifestyle. I felt an emptiness that no amount of sex or shopping could fix. I knew that I couldn't continue to strip for a living and fornicate.

My ex-boyfriend was resisting the idea of me going back home to North Carolina. I convinced him that I would come right back. As proof of my commitment, I left half of my belongings behind. When I came back to my parents' house, everything was different. My younger sister had just got saved, and then my father received Jesus not too long after. The house was full of Christians as they were conducting Bible studies. "Oh no. What have I walked into?" I thought.

The Christians were so friendly and looked so happy. They were always smiling, and I thought they were pretending. "There is no way that someone is that happy all the time," I said to myself. I felt like they were judging me, and I wasn't good enough, so I made sure to avoid them. When they were doing a Bible study downstairs in my parents' living room, and it was time to go to work at the club, I would quickly walk by them looking forward. I avoided making eye contact and zoomed out the door with my suitcase full of outfits.

Around this time, my sister begged me to go to church, but I refused, so she gave me a Bible. I was headed out the door, so I placed it on my passenger seat, and that's where it sat for weeks. One day I woke up and felt doom in the depths of my soul. I just knew something terrible was going to happen. I went on with my normal routine and on my way out of the front door, I heard this voice, "You are going to die today." I didn't realize that the devil was talking to me. As soon as I heard his voice, I felt the spirit of death, and I knew that my end was near.

A few minutes after I left the house, the spirit of death returned. I was blasting music by Chingy and I looked up into my rear-view mirror. I was stopped at the light and barely a few cars were on the road. But what happened next played in slow motion. I could see bright headlights gleaming straight towards me. I said, "This car is not dumb enough to hit me when there is an empty lane right beside me." A few seconds later, the car slammed into the back of me — the lady who was driving pulled over into the median while I was still parked at the light.

To my ignorance, I had no idea that you are supposed to move your car over to the side or out of harm's way in an accident. I remember thinking, "My daddy told me never to move my car in an accident." So, I stayed in the lane. The lady got out of the car and came up to my window. She lightly tapped on it. Then I rolled it down. "I'm sorry. I couldn't brake soon enough. Do you have a black n' mild?"

I felt irritated because this lady is high as a kite, hits my car then has the nerve to ask me for a smoke. "No. I don't," I replied as nicely as I could. The lady calls the police to report the incident while standing near my car. I cut on my hazard lights. As I was leaning forward to get my registration and insurance information out of my glove department, another car slams right into the back of my vehicle.

My car went forward several feet and I thought I had died. My life flashed before my eyes. I jumped out of the vehicle, screaming hysterically. The same lady who hit my car grabbed me and held me. "Are you okay? It's alright!" As she consoled me, I realized that I was still alive and came back into my right mind. I hugged her tightly as I cried. A minute later, I looked over to my left. I saw a car hit the power pole and the driver's legs were hanging outside. I knew he was severely injured because he wasn't moving. Fear gripped me as I thought that he could be dead. Later, I found out that he survived.

I looked at the ground before me and saw my CDs, credit cards, and broken glass scattered across the wet road. I looked at my car and saw the entire backseat smashed in. If anyone were in the rear of the vehicle, then they would have instantly been killed upon impact. I noticed that my face and neck was in pain, so I touched my face only to discover that my eyebrow ring on my left brow came out. As I tried to talk, I realized that my braces had shifted and the colored rubber bands that aligned my teeth popped off. When I tried to move, excruciating pain shot down my back. The pain worsened as the shock wore off.

At that moment, the fireman arrived at the scene. One directed the traffic, and another one swept all the glass and my belongings out of the street. I looked to the right at the fireman standing on the grass near the fire truck. He bent down and picked up the Bible that my sister had given me a few weeks prior. I was shocked at how the Bible had landed several feet away on the grass and not the asphalt. If it had fallen on the road, a car would have driven over it. He said, "Come here, young lady. This book saved your life," while handing me the Bible. He looked at the car and shook his head in disbelief that I survived. Then he said, "Sit down and wait for the ambulance to take you to the hospital."

A few minutes later, the Emergency Medical Transporters came and strapped me to a baseboard and put a brace on my neck. They transported me to the hospital, and I went through a series of tests as they checked for internal damage and broken bones. My family rushed to the hospital and prayed over me. A few hours later, I went home in pain. My face and my back were swollen from the impact. I visited a chiropractor for a whole year before I returned to normal. A week after the accident, one of the Christian ladies who conducted Bible studies at my parents' house invited me over.

She wanted to do a Bible study with me, so I sat down at the kitchen table. She had a small pamphlet about the gifts of the Holy Spirit with the evidence of speaking in tongues. As she went over the lesson, I started to feel tears well up in the corner of my eyes. I felt the exact way that I did months prior when I went to church with my ex-boyfriend and his mother. Only this time, I couldn't suppress the tears because they began to pour like a waterfall.

She looked at me and stopped the lesson. "Do you believe in Jesus Christ?" I nodded my head yes. "Do you want to be saved?" I replied yes. "Do you believe that the gift of speaking in tongues is for you?" "Yes," I sobbed. Suddenly, she stood to her feet and laid her hand on my forehead. My head went back, tears rolled down my face, the power of God surged through my body, and my mouth opened as I cried. I couldn't fight God anymore. I yielded, and He took control. My tongue started flapping violently and I had no clue as to what was happening.

A language that I never spoke of came out of me, and I realized that I had received the gift of speaking in other tongues. A couple of days later, I went to church and got water baptized. I felt so clean and pure inside. I was so happy, and that empty feeling that I had carried around for years disappeared. I knew that I had to stop stripping, so I went to the club and cleaned out my locker and never looked back.

WARNING SIGNS

1. How does your spirit feel?

Even though I wasn't a Christian during the car accident, I was sensitive to the spirit realm. There is another world that we interact with daily that we can't see with our natural eyes. God, Himself is a Spirit, and we interact with Him daily. Sometimes we can feel His presence or hear His voice.

2 Corinthians 3:17 says, "Now the Lord is that Spirit: and where the Spirit of the Lord is, there is liberty."

Even if we can't trace Him by faith, we know He is here because He promises to never leave or forsake us (Deuteronomy 31:6). There are three parts to man, which is the body, soul, and spirit.

1 Thessalonians 5:23 says, "And the very God of peace sanctify you wholly; and I pray God your whole spirit and soul and body be preserved blameless unto the coming of our Lord Jesus Christ."

When our spirit (life or breath) leaves our bodies, then our souls enter eternity. Whether you spend it in heaven or hell depends if you have accepted Jesus as your Savior and if you are in right standing with God. The body is just a shell that will eventually turn to dust.

I knew something wasn't right because my spirit man was able to feel death. It is a dark force that places fear, gloom, and destruction upon anyone who encounters it. I never felt death until the day of the accident and when I did, I knew exactly what it was without someone having to tell me about it. Many people know when their time is coming to an end. They began to make funeral arrangements, their will, power of attorney, and any last requests. I worked in healthcare for a decade and saw many deaths. I knew when my patients would converse with me that if they felt like they would never leave the hospital, then most likely they wouldn't.

2. Devil's voice

When I heard the enemy speak to me, it placed fear and intimidation within me, which are two of the biggest tactics the enemy uses. When you are fearful, then you aren't operating in faith. Without it, then it's impossible to please God (Hebrews 11:6). The just shall live by faith (Romans 1:17), meaning that children of God must have a lifestyle of faith. It's not an option but a requirement.

The enemy will try to cause intimidation to hinder us from realizing who we are in Christ, walking in authority, and fulfilling our destinies. When I heard his voice, fear came over me, and I knew something bad was going to happen.

Over the years, when I suffered from anxiety, the enemy spoke to me daily. He told me how much he hated me and was going to kill me. I was frightened, so I stayed isolated and left the house only to go to work. Even then, I had to withdraw several times during the night to do deep breathing exercises so I wouldn't have a panic attack.

LESSONS LEARNED

1. Don't speed in the rain

You will be surprised at how many people do this. When it rains during cold weather, sleet or ice can form on bridges. Many signs are set along the highway as a warning that the roads are slippery when wet. Adverse weather can cause your vehicle to crash while injuring you and others. It's best to slow down and drive cautiously. The lady who hit me was speeding and couldn't stop in time without hitting me. The second driver who hit me had low visibility because of the rain. It wasn't until he was right up on me that he realized he was about to crash into me.

2. Pull over to the median

During my accident, I was either nineteen or twenty. I was very naive and lacked common sense. When you get in a car accident, please get out of harm's way by pulling on the grass or median. Moving your car to safety won't hinder the crash report from being investigated. You don't want to get rear-ended twice as I did by deciding to stay in the traffic lane. Some people are distracted as they drive by texting. Others are impaired by narcotics like the woman who ran into my car. Use wisdom. If you lack it, then ask God for it. He will give you a generous supply of it (James 1:5). As you grow in Him, He will give you another level of wisdom called sound wisdom (Proverbs 2:7).

3. Don't resist God

I am blessed that the Lord never gave up on me. I ran for a long time and I tried to hide from him. We can't hide anything from God.

Psalms 139:7 (ESV) says, "Where shall I go from your Spirit? Or where shall I flee from your presence? If I ascend to heaven, you are there! If I make my bed in Sheol, you are there!"

His love for us is relentless. Many people don't get another opportunity to accept Jesus into their hearts. I was fortunate enough to have several. Sometimes the chance of receiving salvation doesn't come around often for those who are stuck in certain lifestyles. Jesus Christ is the last person in their minds. The devil's job is to kill, steal, and destroy, but Jesus came to give life more abundantly (John 10:10).

The devil (god of this world) pulls people further away from God and he has blinded their eyes with darkness.

2 Corinthians 4:4 says, "In whom the god of this world hath blinded the minds of them which believe not, lest the light of the glorious gospel of Christ, who is the image of God, should shine unto them."

When I went to church the first time and listened to Fred Hammond's album, I felt God drawing me. However, the enemy snatched me deeper into sin and I resisted the idea of being saved. I continued to sin. The devil knew he had to try to kill me before the Lord started drawing me again. My family and the group of Christians were praying for me — the fervent effectual prayers of the righteous availeth much (James 5:16).

4. Yield to be filled

Many people can't receive the gift of tongues because they have several spirits blocking them. A religious spirit can cause one to analyze everything and try to figure out God. We must have childlike faith (Matthew 18:2-4). Who can understand the mind of God? His ways aren't our ways and His thoughts aren't like our thoughts (Isaiah 55:8). Sometimes a person must unlearn everything before they can receive and operate in the supernatural because their mind was programmed against it.

Fear is another spirit that hinders people from letting go and allowing God to have His way. Some felt afraid and thought people who spoke in tongues were crazy. They put up a barrier and couldn't receive, even though the power of God was present.

Some atmospheres aren't conducive for the Holy Spirit to flow as He desires. Often it takes teaching the Word of God for us to come into the truth of the Gospel to gain a revelation about these gifts. Sign and wonders follow the Word (Mark 16:20).

That day during the Bible study, I felt the presence of the Lord. I couldn't fight Him anymore. I put my hands up as an act of surrender — His will over mines. I yielded to Him and didn't have to tarry for the gift. I was filled instantly.

5. You can't come into agreement

The devil is the father of all lies. There is no truth in him. He was a murderer from the beginning (John 8:44). Many people are bound because they agreed with the devil's lies. "It won't work. Give up. No one loves you. Who is going to support you?" don't listen to this voice because it's the enemy trying to talk you out of what God wants you to do.

When the devil told me, "You are going to die today," I said, "Nah," then shook off that feeling. What would've happened if I agreed? I wouldn't be here today because I would have given him permission to take me out. Agreeing with something is giving it access into your life and spirit. How many people are sick today or quit something they started because they listened to the voice of the enemy?

CHAPTER 14

NEAR DEATH IN THE KITCHEN

By Tréasa Brown

I was a young mother of three children, twenty-three years old, and had not yet accepted Christ as my Lord and personal savior. I was born and raised in the church. I knew I was going to give my life to God, but it was always a matter of when. I had just prepared a hot meal along with some pork-chop steaks. As I began to enjoy my dinner, the meat had been swallowed wrong, went down the wrong pipe, and I began to choke. It caught me by surprise that I was choking like a baby. I managed to get myself to the kitchen and I began to hover over the sink. As I'm trying to cough up the food, numerous thoughts raced through my mind, all in a matter of seconds. As I'm struggling for my life, I thought of a strategy to get the pork-chop steak pieces out of my throat. "Do I swallow or cough this out? Swallowing may cause it to go down the wrong pipe resulting in my air supply being cut off instantly." So, I was afraid of choosing that option. I thought my children or family members were going to find me dead on my kitchen floor. "No one will know about my death until they find me in the morning!"

Death was the focus as I'm choking! I cough out one piece and the struggle started again, as there's still another piece caught in my throat. So finally, I decided to swallow it and bless the Lord, it went down the right way. Afterward, I walked over to my living room couch and desperately gasped for air! At that moment, I said to myself, "I almost died!" Immediately I called my mother and told her about the near-death experience in detail. She told me that while on her way to work, she could've been in a car accident, but it ended up being the person in front of her. She also said that my sister was walking to or from school and almost got hit by a car! The vehicle was several inches away from my sister.

My mind was blown that day because of all the things that were happening all at once. Still, to this day, the thoughts that filled my mind, within seconds were profound. I indeed could've died right there in my sin! The fight was on for my life, right there in a matter of moments. I would often watch the Word Network and see different sermons being preached but would never heed the warnings that the Lord would send my way. There was always conviction as the Lord would tug at my heart. A part of me wanted to hold on to the things of this world, which delayed my salvation. I would pray before I went to bed, acknowledge Him, but I was not in a place to submit to God and give total surrender to His will.

Hebrews 3:7-8 in the first and second part of that stanza declares, "Wherefore as the Holy Ghost saith, Today if ye will hear his voice, Harden not your hearts, as in provocation…"

Once my sister dreamed that the Lord came back and I wasn't ready. As she was relaying her dream to me, I remember her telling me that there was a cloud coming. My sister was trying to warn me that Jesus was coming. She said things like, "Look" or "Tréasa," in getting my attention concerning the cloud. In this dream, I was telling my sister not to worry and how a family member was going to pray for me. But my sister was trying to express the urgency that Jesus was coming, and I didn't seem to be concerned. When she went over the dream, I felt conviction and I was angry! In my mind, I had a list of things that I wanted to do before I got saved, then I would surrender. But seemingly, the Lord had another plan to catch my attention through this message. My sister's dream did something on the inside of me. It caused me to think! Perhaps these were some of the warning signs that the Lord was trying to convey. Jesus loved me enough to catch my attention and this was not the first time that I didn't take heed to Him.

When I finally yielded to Jesus, what stood out to me later about the dream is that my back was turned in the opposite direction of this cloud. When your back is turned, you are caught off guard. I wasn't worried about His coming! I thank God that I didn't see my demise in that kitchen, because if I did, I would've spent eternity in hell. Thank God for multiple chances. I thank Him that He loves His people enough to warn them. You better thank God for another opportunity! So many people take the very breath of God for granted.

The Bible declares in Genesis 2:7, And the LORD God formed man of the dust of the ground, and BREATHED into his nostrils the BREATH OF LIFE; and man became a LIVING SOUL.

Don't miss your opportunity to get it right with God, before He has to catch your attention! Don't take life for granted, but with every breath, you breathe, live for Jesus. You don't have to be near death before He catches your attention. Let go of this world and say "Yes" to Jesus!

WARNING SIGNS FROM A DIFFERENT PERSPECTIVE

1. The Lord tugging on my heart

The Lord always convicts and chastens who He loves. There were many times that He was tugging on my heart.

2. Sermons

Some of the sermons that were being preached through the Word Network caught my attention. Sometimes they brought me to tears and brought forth conviction.

3. My Sister's Dream

My sister's dream caused me to feel conviction and anger, but it was right on time.

LESSONS LEARNED

1. Warning signs are vital and should never be overlooked.
2. Don't harden your heart the day you hear the Lord calling you. Just say, yes!
3. Yield to every warning the Lord is giving you because He loves you.
4. Turn a-loose the things of this world and grab ahold of Jesus.

CHAPTER 15

Crib Death

BY KIMBERLY MOSES

I had sinus problems all my life. I would produce a lot of phlegm that got hard and felt like it was stuck in my throat. Over the years, I dealt with nausea and anxiety as a result. I developed a Menthol addiction to soothe my throat. So, I love to suck on cough drops even though I was not coughing. I don't wish sinus problems on my worst enemy.

From the ages of nine to twelve, my peers would ask me, "Why do you breathe so hard?" My only answer was, "I don't know." I never realized that I was breathing hard until they brought it to my attention. My feelings were hurt because the kids started to treat me differently and didn't want to play with me. Some of them made fun of me.

I was a mouth breather up until I was twelve. One day in the kitchen, I asked my mother, "Momma, why do I breathe so hard?" I was shocked by her response. She told me what happened to me when I was a baby.

"One day, I laid you down in your crib in your room. Some time went by and I went to check on you. When I went into the room and looked in the crib, you weren't breathing. You were turning purple. So, I yelled as panic rushed through me. Greg, Kimberly is not breathing. Your dad rushed into the room, picked you up, holding you with one hand underneath your belly, he took the other and did some upward thrusts on your back. You began to cough and spit up mucus as you cried."

My father was skilled in CPR and the Lord orchestrated his steps to be home that day. Imagine if my father hadn't acted quickly to dislodge the phlegm, then I wouldn't be here today. What if my mother didn't follow her instincts to check on me, then there would be no Kimberly Moses Ministries?

I had no idea that this occurred, and everything started to make sense. Around this time, I remember complaining to my parents almost daily that I couldn't breathe, and my nose was stopped up. I would wake up in the morning and blow my nose so hard, but very little phlegm came out. I would hold down one side of my nostril and blow my nose. At first, this technique seemed to work, but then my sinuses were stuffy again. Having sinus issues was normal to me because that's all I knew. My parents were concerned, so they took me to my primary care physician, who diagnosed me with Hay Fever. He prescribed me a bunch of Claritin and other sinus pills. At that time, I couldn't swallow pills, so my parents crushed them for me.

The pills relieved all my symptoms. So over time, I learned how to swallow the medicine in a tablet form. I knew that I would probably have to take pills to deal with sinuses for the rest of my life, so why not learn since I had recently turned thirteen. My sinus opened and I was amazed at how the air felt going into my nostrils. I would wake up in the morning and I didn't feel like my nose was clogged. My peers around me noticed that my breathing wasn't labored anymore. They asked me to ride bikes and play patty cake with them again. I was happy again.

I feel blessed to be alive because many babies die of crib death or Sudden Infant Death Syndrome (SIDS). They also die of Sudden Unexpected Infant Death (SUID). According to the Center for Disease Control, in 2017, there were 3,600 sudden unexpected infant deaths (SUID) in the United States. These deaths occur among infants less than one-year-old and have no immediately obvious cause.1[27] I bless God for not allowing me to become another statistic. The Lord was protecting me because one day, He would use me to preach His word.

The devil tried to kill me when I was only a few months old. He tried to do the same with Moses and Jesus. They both were prophets or God's divine messenger. In the first two chapters in the Book of Exodus, we can read about the Pharaoh, who was intimidated by how strong the Hebrew slaves were. They were

---

27. "Sudden Unexpected Infant Death and Sudden Infant Death Syndrome." CDC. https://www.cdc.gov/sids/data.htm (Accessed February 2, 2020).

increasing in population and Pharaoh passed a wicked decree to perform genocide. He ordered to throw all male Hebrews that were born into the Nile River. Now think how evil that is. Here innocent lives were murdered for no just cause. The midwives feared God and some of them didn't comply with this heinous law. Moses' birth mother was able to hide her son for three months. We know how much the Lord used Moses, such as using him as a deliverer to rescue the Israelites out of bondage so they could go to the promised land one day. When we read about Moses, we have no other choice but to believe in wonders because he witnessed the supernatural frequently:

- The burning bush (Exodus 3)
- Aaron's staff turning into a serpent (Exodus 7:8-13)
- His hand turning leprous and restored (Exodus 4:6-7)
- The ten plagues (Ex. 11:1–12:36)
- Parting the Red Sea (Exodus 14)
- Water coming from the rock (Exodus 17, Numbers 20)
- Quails (Exodus 16)
- Manna (Exodus 16)
- Glory cloud by day (Exodus 13:21–22)
- Pillar of Fire by night (Exodus 13:21–22)
- Face to Face encounters (Exodus 33:11)
- Supernatural revelation to write the Ten Commandments (Exodus 19, Exodus 24, Deuteronomy 4, Exodus 31:18)

No wonder the devil tried to take out Moses because he was a threat to his kingdom. The enemy thought that if he could kill Moses in his infancy, then he would put a stop to his destiny, but he was very wrong. Moses left a legacy that is still talked about today.

Let's look at another example, which is Jesus. In Matthew 2, we read about the wicked King Herod. After he heard the Wise men say, "Where is he that is born King of the Jews? For we have seen his star in the east, and come to worship him," a malicious plan entered his heart. He wanted to find Jesus so he could kill him. When he realized that the Wise Men tricked him, then he ordered the male children in Bethlehem two or younger to be killed. The enemy knew about the prophecy of Jesus, so he tried to prevent it from coming to pass. However, God the Father, sent an angel to warn Joseph in a dream to flee and not return until Herod's death.

- Jesus is the ultimate example of our faith (1 Peter 2:21-25).
- He is the living atonement for our sins (1 John 2:2).
- He died to save humanity (John 3:16).
- Through Him, we have the gift of eternal life (Romans 6:23).
- He paid the price so we can be healed of our infirmities and live a life of freedom (Isaiah 53:5).
- He ascended on high so the Holy Spirit could come (John 16:7, Ephesians 4:8)

When will the devil learn that he can't stop what God has ordained? How many young prophets or other babies with a call on their life never got a chance to live because of abortion, genocide, or murder was their portion?

WARNING SIGNS

1. Quiet Baby For too long

Being a parent can be a joyful experience, but the reality of having a newborn includes sleepless nights. You must put your schedule around the baby, meaning that you sleep when your infant sleeps. When the baby is hungry two to four hours later, you must wake up to nurse or feed your child. It's good to get in the routine of constantly checking on your child throughout the day. Sometimes, you might have to take a break to do things around the house but be on high alert if you haven't heard your baby coo, cry, pass gas, laugh, or cough for a while. My mother later told me that she didn't hear me making any sounds for a while, so she decided to check on me.

2. Gut feeling

How many times have you had a gut feeling that something wasn't right, but you ignored it only to regret it later? Most likely, that is the Holy Spirit warning you that something isn't right. You may feel an uneasy feeling, restless, or gloomy. Pay attention because usually, when you feel peace about something, it is a good sense. On the other hand, checks in your spirit mean to take heed unless you fall (1 Corinthians 10:12). Most mothers are really attached to their infant child and have an unusual connection. They know when something isn't right, which is called motherly instinct. Not everyone hears the audible voice of God, so He speaks in other ways, such as lifting the sense of peace so you can pray and find out why.

LESSONS LEARNED

The devil hates prophets and will try to kill them. He feels the earlier he can take them out of the world, the better. He will do everything he can to prevent the prophecy from coming to pass by trying to annihilate a child of God. The word of God will be fulfilled and what His chosen vessel is called to do shall surely happen. No weapon formed against us shall prosper (Isaiah 54:17). The devil is defeated, and Jesus is Lord.

CHAPTER 16

Domestic Violence

BY STEPHANIE HAM

My next near-death experience occurred in 1989. At that time, I was older and not living for the Lord. I thought I was in love with a stripper named Dingo. During this time, I was working as a construction worker. I lived on Empire and Kingston Avenue in Crown Heights, Brooklyn, NY. I woke up one night from a deep sleep by sounds coming from the living room. My boyfriend was having sex with someone else. I lost my mind. We got into a fight. Dingo went to the kitchen, grabbed out a knife, and put it to my throat. He was holding me back from attacking the girl so that she could escape. After she left out, you would have thought there were two men in the house fighting. Thank God for my next-door neighbor who heard all the commotion going on, so they decided to call the cops. Before the police arrived, he was nowhere to be found. "How could he?" I said out loud.

Death was staring me right in the face that night. I hated my ex-boyfriend for what he did to me. I probably would have killed him especially when he came back three weeks later to apologize. I had a five-year-old son to raise and I did not want him coming to see me in Rikers Island. Whenever I would go through something, I would find myself crying and calling on God. We do the darndest things when we think we're in love. I went to get a reading from a psychic, so they could tell me about Dingo. One thing in life is that we should all always call on God when we need Him to solve our problems. But often we do not realize that we need Jesus as our Lord and Savior. After everything Dingo did, I still went back to him. Yes, I know! I was foolish for going back. I was even deceived into thinking that I could manipulate God to get this man to love me.

When we broke up, the grim reaper came into my house. He was walking down the hallway. When he walked past the kitchen, the cabinets opened up and glasses and china fell out of the cabinet. I had to put worship music on and pray to God. Around this time, I was caught up in being a Black Jew. I told the grim reaper, "Flee in the name of Jesus." He looked at me and laughed. He said, "You have no power!" He turned around and walked away

Ultimately, Dingo and I were not supposed to be together and this relationship dissolved. We came in contact one last time at a club. He saw me and I did what Dionne Warwick says to do,

"Every time you see me walking down the street, just walk on bye."

WARNING SIGNS

He was conniving and unfaithful. The first warning sign occurred when my house was broken into from the inside out. He robbed me. I was naive and didn't want to believe that a man that I was dating could do such a thing. When I came into the house on the day of the robbery, I was looking for my curling iron. I had called the cops because my clothes and other stuff were all over the place. I used to be a construction worker, so the Lord blessed me to have the finest of clothes that I desired. I couldn't find my leather coat with the fur around it. I couldn't find a lot of my good quality clothes. Many people die each year from domestic violence. I was blessed to walk away.

The next warning sign was when he had a party in our apartment, and I didn't know about it until my best friend told me. She told me that there were a lot of strange people in my house. Remember that I was just robbed.

LESSONS LEARNED

1. Don't Ignore the Warning Signs.

Don't ignore the warning signs when they are given to us because they are there for a reason. If a man wants to leave you, then let him go. I didn't want him to go and there were so many warning signs and I ignored them. I was caught up in who he was and how he pulled me out of my shell. I thought it was cool to date a stripper. Another warning sign was given to me while dating Dingo. I came home and approached my door to unlock it. However, my bottom lock was locked. That was odd because we never locked that part of the door and it meant I couldn't open the door. When I came up to the door, I heard moaning sounds and there was a man inside that he claimed was his cousin. I think that he was on the down low. I should have listened to my instincts instead of giving him any more chances.

2. Seek God for Direction.

I tried to keep him in my life by going to a psychic. I put one hundred dollars in the Bible and had her tell me something about my ex: whether we were going to get married or stay together. When I went to get a reading from the psychic, I felt an evil spirit. She gave me some potion to put in my bathwater. When I used to put it in my bath, it tore up my stomach and gave me bad cramps. My spirit told me not to put the potion in my water anymore after doing it twice. I threw it away and when I did, things started to happen. He never stayed with me and I woke up to him having sex with another woman. Once you open demonic portals in your life, it will take the power of Jesus to close it. Going to psychics opens up the gateway for the enemy to enter your life.

3. Look for love in God.

. When you are hurt and wounded and looking for love, you will tolerate a lot of things and ignore the truth. You will keep

hoping the man will change. I should have trusted the love of God rather than a destructive person.
.

***

DOMESTIC VIOLENCE

BY ALLENA DOUGLAS

My drive and ambition to succeed in life became fierce. My mantra was, "I can do all things through Christ strengthens me." I went to college on a scholarship to play basketball. My schedule was very rigorous. I had a full load of classes, daycare, practices, homework, and parenting. I attended a non-denominational church, where I started to develop an intimate relationship with God.

One day I met a big strong football player. We were instantly attracted to one another. We dated for a brief period and six months later, we were married. After a short honeymoon, Coach Eddie Robinson owned the apartments for married students and assisted us. We acclimated to parenting and schooling but easily became overwhelmed. My husband became short tempered and began to drink. He later became possessive and would challenge men for looking at me or becoming close to me. I noticed that he raised his voice a lot, and I would become easily startled. I would always try to make good with him because I was afraid. Playing basketball, class schedule, and parenting, left a little time to work a job. I was offered a wonderful opportunity to model. The money was good and helped our household. My husband continued to get increasingly jealous and then accused me of wanting other men. I tried to reassure him that I didn't love anyone but him.

My husband continued to drink, and his behavior became more erratic. His father died, and he was very depressed. I tried to support him the best that I knew how. One day he came home early from practice. I asked him, "Are you okay? Did you get hurt?" He stated "No, I quit." I asked him what his plans were and that we should have discussed the decision. That was the start of the beatings. I went to class with black eyes and bruises. When asked what happened, I would make excuses such as "I got elbowed in the eye or face in basketball practice," or "I fell in practice." The beatings became more frequent. I became isolated to the point where my grades began to suffer, and my scholarship was in jeopardy. I prayed that my marriage would get better.

We dropped out of college to move with my husband's family in Lake Charles, Louisiana. Initially, things were great. We attended church, worked and started saving money with plans to return to college. Despite working, my husband returned to his old ways of hanging out and drinking. My time was spent with my children, his family, and at church. I tried to help financially, clean-up, but I didn't dare cook. My cooking skills were subpar. My mother-in-law taught me how to make Cajun cuisine. My husband's family was supportive. However, his mother verbalized being displeased with our relationship and her son's behavior. I met some women who were helping with my spiritual walk with God. My prayer life had increased and so had my relationship with God. I knew as a child of God, my children and I deserved better. I told my husband that I was pregnant. He continued with the beatings and stayed out late at night.

Shortly after having our new baby, I called my mother to tell her about the abuse. She drove to get us. My husband's mother had called her pastor and the police to keep me from leaving with the children. My husband took my newborn son (Ted) from me. I begged and pleaded for him to give me the baby. Out of desperation, I retrieved my mom's gun from her car and demanded my child. The two police officers drew their weapons on me. The police stated, "Put the gun down." I was sobbing. All I wanted was my baby. My brother Robert was my angel. He was only in high school. He jumped in between me and the police and said, "Lena put the gun down. Ray, give her the baby." I have never felt such a calming presence. I believe the Holy Spirit took control of a moment that could have turned fatal for me and others. God stepped in and dispatched his warring angels to protect us on that day. I was distraught and crying. I had put myself in a dangerous position. I thanked God for his goodness.

I returned home with the full support of my family. I worked very hard and attended school. My children were growing up and they missed their father. I continued to pray for my husband. We reconciled then moved to Fort Lewis Washington Army Base with hopes to start our lives over in our new careers. Washington State was beautiful. The kids were happy and loved school. We were doing well at our new jobs. One of the captains had invited my family to church. We went and to my surprise, my husband said, "Let's join." I didn't pray about it because

I thought God was answering my prayers. We joined the New Testament Church and Christian Servicemen's Home. We went to church 5-7 times a week. The more we attended, the more I questioned what we were being taught. Pastor Mitchell taught that women were to go to their husbands. He preached that men needed to get their wives in order and men are the head of their households.

Ephesians 5:23 says, "For the husband is head of the wife, as also Christ is head of the church; and He is the Savior of the body." My husband thought this permitted him to start abusing me again. I lived on the altar, praying and asking God why? I went to work and was frequently questioned about the bruises or black eyes. However, I made excuses. My husband left the church, started hanging out with his friends, drinking, and was seen with other women. The beating intensified.

I continued to go and take my children to church because I felt safe. As I continued to pray and ask God about things, the more revelation I received. My eyes and ears opened because the things being taught in church didn't line up. I went to talk to pastor Mitchell and his wife regarding the abuse I was experiencing and the questions I had about what he was teaching. I showed him the bruises. I told him how afraid my children and I were for our lives. I asked questions about Scriptures and had told him about what I felt the Holy Spirit was speaking to me. The pastor basically told me I was defying him.

I was told in Corinthians 7:14 that the unbelieving husband has been sanctified through his wife. And the unbelieving wife is sanctified by the husband. Elsewhere the children were unclean but now they are holy.

I believed in my heart that God didn't want me to stay in this abusive relationship. I went to talk to Army Chaplain Harris. I was totally transparent about the abuse, my church life, my home life, and my son's medical condition. Chaplain Harris provided counseling and household assistance with a compassionate reassignment based on Ted's medical needs and the lethality of my abuse. Chaplain Harris left me with one scripture. 1 John 4:8: Whoever does not love does not know God, because God is love.

I took my children back home to Louisiana to my mother and my grandmother, where they wouldn't have to witness anymore abuse. We could have been killed but thank you, Jesus, for keeping us safe.

One night, my husband broke into my home because he had pending charges for the things he had done. I was still awaiting processing to be completed where I could go to Fort Polk, Louisiana and I had a few more weeks to complete school. He told me he was there to kill me. He committed some horrible acts that night. He continually beat me in my face while saying, "I will make it where no one will want you. If I can't have you, then no one will." God saved me because the police knocked on the door. I didn't answer. They came in and arrested him. I went to Madigan Army Hospital. Captain Smith in the ER stated that he was tired of me coming to the ER with bruises and not pressing charges. He stated, "I am going to numb your face good. I will do plastic stitches, so the scar isn't too bad."

Today, that scar is still visible under my left eye. It makes my face somewhat asymmetrical because of the extent of the injury. I almost died, But GOD SAVED ME. My facial bones were crushed, which also caused some dental issues due to a jawbone injury. But I count it all joy! My beauty hasn't diminished because Jesus lives on the inside of me and His love overflows to my outer countenance.

I returned to Louisiana and played basketball at Fort Polk. I was granted a wonderful internship at St. Patrick's Hospital in Lake Charles, Louisiana. I worked on the weekends and stayed in the Nun's Parsonage. My goal was to regain my life and to get divorced. My husband returned home and learned that I was in Lake Charles working. He tried to win me back by bringing gifts to the hospital. I turned them down and this infuriated him. He soon started to hide in the parking garages and assaulted me. I told my supervisor, Joe, that I was afraid of him and the attacks. We prayed before my shift was over. Joe was an overweight medium height white man. My husband was in the parking lot. Joe had no fear. He told him, "Get behind thee Satan. The fire of God will rain down on you if you touch her or harm her. I call from heaven a host of warring Angels to come on her behalf right now in the mighty name of Jesus." He became afraid and walked away. I almost died, but God was yet merciful.

I moved to Ft Polk Army Base, where I played for the basketball team and commuted to Lake Charles for work. My faith increased and I believed the Scripture Philippians 4:13, I can do all things through Christ who strengthens me. I began to attend church services at The Post Chapel and met wonderful people who encouraged my children and I. After spending time in prayer on this specific day, I felt the presence of the Holy Spirit. I had finally found the courage to file for divorce.

I took the children to visit with their father and to get the rest of our household goods. The visit initially went well. I continued to pack things as my children visited. I began to leave, and my husband said, "No." I politely stated, "We are going through a divorce. I want to get my things and the children so we can leave." I started to pray. He pulled out a sawed-off shotgun, pushed me down on the ground, putting the gun to my head. He said, "I will not let anyone else have you." My children were crying and screaming, begging, "No, daddy! No, daddy, please daddy! Don't hurt my mommy!" I prayed and cried for God's protection. I prayed that my children's lives would be spared. I heard in my spirit, "You shall live and not die." Suddenly there was a knock at the door. His friend came to the home and immediately realized something was wrong. As I prayed, I heard the audible voice of God saying, "leave!" I almost died! God spared my children and me.

WARNING SIGNS

- My husband was quick tempered. He started to drink and stay out.
- My husband's behaviors escalated over the years.
- We were not equally yoked.

LESSONS LEARNED

- I learned the importance of praying and asking God about every area of my life.
- I learned how important it was to have a relationship with God. He who has an ear let him hear. I listened to my pastor despite what God was telling me.
- I learned that I could pray and there is nothing impossible with God. However, that person must want to change. God offers salvation at freewill.
- I learned that I didn't know how to get free because of tradition, religiosity, and fear of failure. Domestic violence almost cost me my life. I didn't die, but my children and I will always be affected.

CHAPTER 17

Drowning

BY JALONZO SAMUELS

At the age of fourteen, my father, mother, and I went on a church picnic at Santee State Park. It was a hot summer day. The sky was beautiful with a wonderful atmosphere. We had the usual: fried chicken, potato salad, and the works. You know how we do it. At the park, there is a large lake where one could swim, ride the paddle boats, or just enjoy the coolness of the water. Well, there was a large diving board in the middle of the lake which you had to swim out to. I did not have a problem swimming out to the driving board because I was an excellent swimmer. I spent most of the morning swimming back and forth to the diving board diving off of the high board, because I love to swim.

After an hour or so of swimming, I went back to the picnic area to get some of that good old-fashioned home-cooked food and I ate to my heart's desire. After I got full, my mother told me to not go back into the water until my food had digested properly. I told her that I would, but I didn't. There I was back in the water swimming back to the diving board, flipping to the water off of the high board, over and over again. She sent my father to look for me, he saw me on the platform of the diving board and beckoned for me to come back to shore and I obeyed. When I got back to shore, I got reprimanded pretty good by my parents. But hey I was fourteen and we all know how it is when you are young. You think that you know everything, especially after you start smelling yourself a little bit.

So, there I went back into the water, back to the diving board, I snuck on the diving board, jumped high and drove into the water. Well, this time when I drove into the water, I went deeper and deeper until when I looked, all I could see was darkness. No matter how I tried to swim back up to the surface, I went down deeper and deeper. I felt that I would not make it back to the top, I had run out of breath, had become tired. I knew that life was over for me, my life flashed in front of me. With my last breath, I cried to the Lord. I said, "Lord, Please don't let me die like this!" God heard my cry. I felt hands underneath my feet, and they pushed me up from the depths of that watery grave to the surface...GOD SAVED ME! He heard my cry. He once again did not allow death to have victory over me. Once I got to the surface, I sat on the platform for over an hour, just thanking God. In my very young spirit, the Spirit of God reminded me of my age (14) and told me that my mother was (14) when she gave me life. All I could say was, "Thank You, Lord." I caught a ride back to shore with someone on one of the paddle boats and hugged my mother and father. They kept asking me what was wrong with me. I just told them that I loved them, for that's all that I could say...

WARNING SIGNS

I received several warnings in my pursuit to do what I thought was right. The wisdom of my parents, who understood that I was too young to fully understand the dangers of doing things on my own, which could bring a threat of death.

LESSONS LEARNED

Obedience is better than sacrifice, which is a statement that not only applies to the spiritual but also to the natural things of life as well. Had I taken heed to the instructions that were afforded to me, the opportunity for death would have been aborted. But again, God's Grace, Mercy, His Sovereignty outweighed the plan of the enemy. Psalm 91:11-12 states that God would give His angels charge over us to keep us in all of our ways, that they will bear us up in their hands that we will not dash our feet against a stone. As I stated that when I cried out to the Lord against my apparent death, His angels raised me up over death and caused the plan of the enemy to be destroyed.

CHAPTER 18
Fibroids

TERRORIZED BY FIBROIDS

BY EMELIA ADJEI

It would be an understatement to say I nearly died since I felt I died twice and regained my consciousness, and came back to life. Thank God for securing my life to share this testimony. "I'll shall not die but live and will proclaim what the Lord as done" (Ps 118.7). I'm thankful to God to be alive!! I teared up as I was writing, replaying in my mind the near-death scenarios. It was so surreal!! Terrorized might sound like a strong word to describe a medical condition but that's how I felt and lived for a decade with fibroids. I lived in fear, pain, and anguish!!

Thank God for securing my life to share this testimony. It started with one fibroid and over the years, seven more developed. That's a lot in a womb. I looked bloated, usually weak and tired. My periods were heavy, gashing blood, excruciating pain, words can't describe it. I became anemic due to so much blood loss during my periods. Every month was torture and I dreaded as my periods got closer because it was going to be excruciating pain for days. This affected my mood and energy. The agonizing intense period cramps made me cry and roll on the floor, feeling helpless. It felt like a scraper was being used inside my abdomen. The pain was sharp and deep that my entire being was restless. I'm was unable to eat for days because I felt nauseated and threw up several times. Though pain killers were helpful, it got to a point where it didn't reduce the pain and symptoms. One day, the pain was so unbearable that I nearly called 911 because I was out of breath and couldn't endure the pain. This wasn't normal. It was a demonic affliction.

The first-near death incident happened in 2017 at midnight. I woke up to use the bathroom since I felt like throwing up. I knelt by the toilet bowl and as I leaned my head over, I blacked out!! It happened so fast!! All I can remember was everything seem dark and my head was spinning around. It happened so fast!! I couldn't breathe or move and was struggling to open my eyes. I felt something touched me and I regained consciousness. I was terrified!! I knew what had happened. I partially died and came back alive. Oooohhh my God!! I got up and looked in the mirror and saw bruises on my forehead from my head, spinning in the toilet bowl. I was scarily shocked!! I went to lay down, replaying in my mind what had happened. I was terrified.

I fell asleep for few hours and awoke with a Scripture from Psalms 91:5 – "You'll not fear the terror of night, nor the arrow that flies by day." It was the first time I woke up with a Scripture and remembered it. I was being reminded by the Holy Spirit not to be afraid of the threat of the devil. Then I heard in my spirit that the enemy wanted to create a death scene that I committed suicide: a shameful death. My body would have been found with my head inside the toilet bowl. The devil is a liar!! I won't die a disgraceful death until God calls me to heaven.

The second near-death incident happened a few months after the first one. It was early in the morning. The cramps became intense. I had forgotten the pain medicine in the kitchen, so I went downstairs. As I grabbed the medication, I felt like I was lifted and dropped on the floor. Once again, it happened so fast!! I was on the floor, numb, unable to breathe, and everything seemed dark. I was fighting to get up from the floor, but I felt my body being pushed down. It was a spiritual attack that had manifested physically. By God's grace, I regained power and consciousness. I woke up. and I felt like I transcended to another realm of darkness. As I touched my lips, my hands were covered with blood because when I fell, my teeth hit the floor. I went upstairs to rinse my mouth. As I looked in the mirror, I saw scratches around my neck and shoulders. I realized the warning and caution given in Ephesians 6:12, "For we wrestle not against flesh and blood but against principalities, against powers, against rulers of the darkness of this world, against spiritual wickedness in high places."

The Lord fulfilled His word by securing my life, "Many are the afflictions of the righteous, but the Lord delivers us out of them all ~ Ps 34:19. My life was not just preserved to exist on earth but I am here for a purpose, which is to testify the goodness of the Lord and make a difference in the world. I value and treasure life because it's so fleeting. We should all strive to live our best lives, pursue purpose, and seek God, the giver of life.

I should have taken my Christian life seriously since the devil was after me. In Matthew 22:44, "The Lord said to my Lord, sit at my right hand, until I put your enemies under your feet?" I should have engaged in worship for my healing since it promised in Exodus 23:25, "You shall worship the Lord your God, and I will bless your bread and water; and I will take sickness away from among you."

I should have relentlessly prayed for my healing. "O Lord my God, I cried to you for help, and you have healed me." (Psalm 30:2). God will not abandon us when we call on Him. "For he has not despised or abhorred the affliction of the afflicted, and he has not hidden his face from him, but has heard, when he cried to him." (Psalms 22:24).

WARNING SIGNS

According to Medical News Today, fibromyoma, usually referred to as fibroids are abnormal growths that develop in or on a woman's uterus. These tumors can vary in size of a bean to being as large as a melon. Fibroid causes severe abdominal cramps, heavy prolonged periods, anemic, constipation, pelvic and back pains. Depending on the complexity and position in the uterus, fibroids lead to infertility and cause miscarriage. Fibroids affect around forty percent of women by age thirty-five and severity varies. Once a fibroid develops, it can continue to grow until menopause then shrink.

There are no specific causes of fibroid except linked to genetics and growth hormones. There is no cure but various treatments such as laser, surgery and natural treatment. I believe the devil increases the severity to afflict and torment women. God does not willingly afflict or grieve His children, according to Lamentations 3:33, "For he does not willingly bring afflictions or grief to anyone."

LESSONS LEARNED

After I had surgery to remove the fibroids, I heard testimonies of women being healed supernaturally. Isaiah 53:5 assured that "By His stripes we're healed." God is healer if we seek and believe in him. God is the ultimate protector and giver of life. After my first incident, I should have been serious and committed with my walk in the Lord, but I was lukewarm. The enemy gained ground to continue to afflict and torment me. I later realized that my life was on the line. The devil was after me to die. I got serious with prayer, faith, fear and love of God grew. I knew that my life was in God's hands and He had the final say. "It is good for me that I was afflicted, that I might learn your statutes." (Psalm 119:71).

Being alive is a precious, priceless gift. Giving a second chance to live is a ticket to pursue purpose, which is the reason you were created to exist on earth. I want my life to be meaningful, make a difference in the world by being of service to others, such as the poor and less privileged. Most importantly, to win souls for the kingdom of God by sharing His goodness and love for all who are willing to follow Him.

I should have sought medical treatment sooner when the fibroids were growing and getting larger. I should have discussed treatment options with my gynecologist. There are natural remedies with herbs that shrink the fibroids and reduces the pain and anemic. I should have taken iron tablets and incorporated more green leafy vegetables in my diet. Also, lifestyle changes can enhance the quality of life and help improve some of the symptoms associated with fibroids: changes such as eating a healthy diet, getting regular exercise, and using relaxation techniques. I should have eaten foods that contain vitamins such as oily fish like salmon or tuna. Vegetables and soya products were less likely to cause uterine fibroids. Research shows a diet high in red meat, high calories, fat, and sugar may be more likely to develop fibroids. Replacing red meat (beef, ham, or lamb) with white meat (chicken or turkey) may help. According to the American Heart Association, meat contains high levels of saturated and trans fats.

I am always filled with tears of joy and gratitude when I recall the two incidents that nearly took my life, but Jehovah Shammah was close with me. God am grateful!!

CHAPTER 19

Flesh

BY MICHELLE LOATMAN

When we think of death, we often limit it to only two categories. However, if we truly take the time to delve into the Bible, we will see there are many different forms of death that can take place. One that stands out to me, in particular, and one that we often overlook, is by means of our flesh. Even as Christians, we can all recall an instance when we have unknowingly or willingly chosen to give into the lust of our flesh and choose the path of our own desires. We often get impatient, fearful, doubtful, and even have the wrong mindset that can lead us out of the will of God. There are also times when dysfunction has been a way of life for us. Children live what they learn. As parents, we model for our children what we expect to see. Or do we? Either way, children will most likely do what they see their parents do, in spite of what they say.

"Traumatic experiences can initiate strong emotions and physical reactions that can persist long after the event. Children may feel terror, helplessness, fear, or physiological reactions such as heart pounding, vomiting, or loss of bowel or bladder control. Children who experience an inability to protect themselves or who lacked protection from others to avoid the consequences of the traumatic experience may also feel overwhelmed by the intensity of physical and emotional responses." [28]

This generational curse can either continue to get passed down to the next generation, or you can decide that the buck stops with you! We are charged with transforming the renewing of our minds through spending time in the Word of God. As an adult, we can no longer blame our choices on our childhood. In order to get truly liberated, you have to pull up your boot straps, buckle your seat belt, and do the work necessary for change. There's nothing impossible with God, once you surrender your will.

For the longest time, I didn't have the skills necessary for Christian dating. I just thought two people were attracted to one another, start dating, and see how things go. Sometimes they work out, sometimes they don't. Boy was I wrong. I didn't know that you had to be equally yoked. I wasn't taught that marriage was a ministry, and the foundation was for God's purpose

---
28. The National Child Traumatic Stress Network (NCTSN)
Retrieved from: https://www.nctsn.org/what-is-child-trauma/about-child-trauma

to be accomplished throughout the journey. Sure we went to church when we were kids, but we also saw those same grownups partying on the weekends, living with people they weren't married to, drinking, smoking, etc. It wasn't out of the ordinary to hear people make foolish remarks like, "Well I love God and God loves me, so," or "God is a forgiving God, He understands when we sin." The famous saying was, "Do as I say, not as I do." But I can tell you as a mother of three, who has made far too many mistakes in her life, that your children follow your example. And your example can save your children, or open the door to demons they are not equipped to handle. I confess, even when I got to a point, I knew most of the Word, learned to understand the voice of God, the prompting of the Holy Spirit, and I still chose to do my own thing.

I remember a couple of years after my divorce and I was in my Word more than I had ever been, but still not enough as I should have been. I was single and trying hard to stay focused. My heart was guarded and I had no interest in letting anyone into my life. I felt like something new was on the horizon and my kids and I had kind of plateaued in life. We had just overcome some pretty big obstacles and were happy to finally be out of a storm. This is where you never want to be too comfortable. You can best believe that even if you don't learn the lessons, the devil is studying you. He learns the lessons you learn, what you like, what you'll say no to at this point, and he uses it as an arsenal in the battle against you. He will save what he has gathered from you from the variety of storms in your life, and save them for just the right time to strike: when you are comfortable, varying in time spent in your Word, and drought in your prayer life. This is a recipe for enemy strikes. No doubt about it!

I remember it just like it was yesterday. I had just got the kids settled and had laid my head down on the pillow to watch my favorite television show while scrolling on Facebook. I received a message in my inbox from someone on my friend's list. We chatted back and forth for over an hour. He had the ability to make me laugh and seemed interesting. Before I knew it, we exchanged numbers and were on the phone all night until 7 am. I was caught off guard. As I look back now, I realized I wasn't on my post, because if I was I would have paid better attention to the kinds of questions he was asking, his responses, and what was really happening. He was feeling me out to get information. He appeared friendly and generous. I gave up too much too soon. Within four days of talking to him, my gut feeling told me something was off. He would call at his convenience, but mainly to check and see what I was doing, and who I was with. The majority of the time he was texting. I am not much of a texter. I prefer talking with someone in person or directly. I want to see your body language, your eyes, how you react or respond to things. I want to observe how you treat others, how you talk to people, how you respond when you get mad. I called his phone and he didn't answer, but he texted right back. I told him up front that I prefer talking on the phone and that texting all the time was for high school. I knew what I wanted, or so I thought, and I didn't want to settle and waste more time on false starts. He pretty much cursed me in Ebonics. I was so mad and shocked at the same time. Nevertheless, I erased his number and moved on. A month in a half later, I get a random text late at night, "Hey stranger." I knew who it was, but I wanted to act like I didn't care. So I text back, "Who dis?" When he recognized his bait wasn't going to work, he just replied, "nevermind." I laughed it off and went to bed. A couple of days went by, I am driving to work and I get a message in my inbox from him, "You really hurt my feelings." If I was smart, I would have run and never looked back. But I didn't.

He would call every night once I got the kids to sleep and we would talk late into the night. He knew how to give just enough of his crumbs to keep the bait dangling in my ignorance. I continued to allow myself to be distracted, even though I knew the Holy Spirit had warned me the first couple days of talking with him, that he was not the one. Once again, I look back now and notice how he chose to deal with me when it was convenient for him. By June he was making plans to come to visit me. But I had to go get him because he didn't have a car, a steady job and he lived with his family. I drove an hour back to our hometown to get him and bring him back to my current state to stay for the weekend. But I wasn't paying attention to the fact that it was his birthday. When we went out he complained about prices and food. I noticed I had an uneasy feeling when he said he didn't really drink much, but he had a couple of drinks each time we went out. The next day as I was bringing breakfast in the room, I walked in on him quickly turn his phone over as if he had just gotten caught doing something. I felt an empty pit in my stomach like I had just made a big mistake. But I continued to override it. By the end of the weekend, he went home.

Some days he would reach out to me and others he would text here and there. One minute it felt like he was interested and the next it felt like he was pulling away. I started to feel confused and it felt very familiar to me. I felt like I had been down this path before. Throughout the next couple of months, there were many, many red flags that the Holy Spirit showed me. He would say one thing and do another. He would play the victim when he would talk about how his last relationships ended. He would be transparent one minute and then next pull away. When he was home he was becoming more and more distant. I think I cut him off two or three times within seven months. On Thanksgiving, we went to his family's house and they were all taking pictures. I noticed every time his family tried to take our picture, he would dip off and go do something or ask me if I wanted to go outside. Eventually, his aunt snapped a picture of us and he was so distant. When I got home later that night and looked at the picture on Facebook, I noticed my daughter and I were in the picture, and he was over to the side like we were in the room together, but not together. That weekend, I asked him why after seven months of being together, going on vacations as a family, attending each other's family events, he still didn't acknowledge me on Facebook. I asked him what we were doing. His response was, "What do you mean, we are seeing each other." Little did he know, because we came from the same hometown, and I had people in my current city who knew him and his people, I knew more than he thought I did.

At this point, I had had several warnings from God in my dreams that something was wrong. Whenever he would come, I had a hard time sleeping. I had started backsliding to my old habits, missing church. I had no prayer life and I can't remember the last time I was in my Word. When he got out of the car that night, little did I know this was the last time I would talk to him for some time. Days went by and I hadn't heard from him. Usually, I would have called and texted him to find out where he was located but I was tired of chasing and forcing things. I went on about my business. A couple of days later I got into an accident and one of his family members told him. He text me and said, "Well I haven't heard from you in days, so I guess it's over and hopefully we can still be friends." I was so mad. He acted like I meant nothing to him and things between us were no big deal. The one thing I forgot to remind myself of was a saying my pastor always said: "When you don't understand the purpose of a thing, abuse is inevitable." (Pastor Anthony Bailey) I understand that now to be, neither one of us understood my worth, nor did he know his. If we had he wouldn't have been treating me that way, and I would not have allowed him to. We teach people how to treat us. Now, this should have been enough to make anyone tired enough to run away. But not me, I just had to keep giving chance after chance.

I packed all of his belongings up in a box and shipped it to him. I didn't want any more hurt, pain, or confusion. I didn't reach out to him and I ignored him every time he tried to reach out to me. That lasted about a month and a half. He started texting me back to back. Saying he was going through something and was about to be homeless. He said that he had been through a lot since not talking to me and needed support. He begged and begged until stupid me allowed him back into my life. I went and picked him up and he poured out his problems to me. Again, ladies, the devil studies you. He knows what you want to hear, how uncomfortable and impatient you are getting. He even studies your prayers. He doesn't know everything about you. Only God knows that. But he is paying attention, even when you're not. At the time I let him back, we were in the middle of a corporate fast. I was supposed to be going to a visiting church to see a prophet friend of mine preach. Well, needless to say, that didn't happen. And I broke my fast.

"No temptation has overtaken you except such as is common to man; but God is faithful, who will not allow you to be tempted beyond what you are able, but with the temptation will also make the way of escape, that you may be able to bear it." (1 Corinthians 10:13, NKJV)

God had given me warning, after warning, after warning. He had given me a way out time and time again. And yet and still I was on my way to destruction and death, by my own hands. What I wasn't paying attention to was taking my children, my God-given purpose and assignments with me. And for what? I saw so much potential in this person. But God showed me his heart and motives time and again and I ignored it. "There is a way that seems right to a man, but its end is the way of death." (Proverbs 14:12)

He moved in with me and got a job, which was helpful for paying the bills. But I was about to truly see the detrimental effects it had on my family, and myself spiritually and physically. He would go out and stay out till late or go home every other weekend. After a while, he started going home and not answering his text or phone calls the entire weekend. And would come home Sunday and act like he should be mad because I was mad. When I would try and put my foot down and demand respect, it would only make matters worse. Over the next couple of months, I got a chance to see him angry, disrespectful to others while we were out, disrespectful to me and how his moods would change. Sometimes he would come home and he was just different. His walk, talk, behavior, and even his smile was different. He started talking about getting a house and having separate bedrooms. At times he would go out after work and not come home till 2, 3, 4 am in the morning and stay out in the living room on the couch all night. Things just kept getting worse and worse. I would give and he would take. I felt depleted. I could see the effect it was having on my kids. Every time I got the nerve up to try and leave him, something would keep drawing me back. When he would do certain things, or have certain people over, I would get a sick feeling in my stomach. One day he brought his best friend to my house. I knew the entire time something wasn't right, but I couldn't put two and two together. The minute I walked in the door I felt so sick. As the night went on the feeling got worse until eventually, I was throwing up. By the end of the night his entire demeanor toward me had changed and I could feel myself getting ready to snap. I was so enraged. This feeling was all too familiar for me. I just couldn't kick it.

One night after work and picking my daughter up from dance class, we were in the drive-thru at McDonald's. And he was acting very strange. He went to hand my daughter an ice cream in the third-row seat and she kept telling him she couldn't reach it. He wasn't paying attention and it slipped out of his hands before she could fully grasp it and dropped on the seat of his truck. He was so angry. He started cursing at both of us, grabbed the ice cream and flung it across my face and out my passenger side window. There was chocolate all over. I was so embarrassed and angry that he was treating us like this. I was madder at myself for allowing it. I can put up with just about anything, but it hurt me to see my kids hurting. As we were driving home, he kept trying to talk to me, I ignored him and told him to just shut up and get us home. He got mad because I wouldn't talk to him and let him grab my hand, so he pulled alongside the road, started speeding through traffic and through red lights on a major highway. I was afraid for my daughter, but I was so angry and so tired of hurting I didn't care what happened to me that night. I told him I wanted him to pack his things and get out of my house within the next 24 hours. I had had enough. He went out to his truck and sat there, texting me ignorant, demeaning, and derogatory things for hours.

The next day, he came back into the house like nothing had happened and tried to take us out to dinner. I refused. So he left for the weekend. He came begging back that Sunday. And I let him stay. I told him how I felt he was disrespecting me and my children, and that his behavior was suspicious. I put my demands on the table and he agreed to do better. Not even a month later and he was back out for the weekend. I remember laying on the couch and dozing off. I thought I was dreaming at first. But I couldn't see anything. I tried waking myself up but couldn't. I could hear and feel my daughter trying to wake me up, but I couldn't get up. But one thing I could do was hear and feel in the spirit. I was asleep physically, but God had taken my spirit where he was located. He was showing me what he was doing, some of the people he was around and things he was doing in my absence. He was warning me of the heightened danger that was coming. When he came home, we went out to eat. But instead of coming to the house he dropped us at the door and said he would be back. He left for a couple of hours, claiming to be with a buddy from work. I woke up in the middle of the night to a text on my phone meant for another woman.

The next morning, I went to take my daughter to school and when I confronted him, he went crazy. He started screaming, grabbed me by my throat, in front of my daughter and slammed me into the wall and front door. I fought him off of me and told him to be gone by the time I got home. I took my daughter to school and when I came back home, he was asleep in my bed like nothing had ever happened. I slammed the closet door open to start packing his belongings, and he got up and started yelling. I told him, "Either you are going outta here or one of us is going out of here in a body bag, but it won't be me." It's time for you to go. I could feel the spirit of murder all around me. I felt like I was about to lose everything. I felt so out of control and so out of touch with God. Once I started throwing his things out of the closet, he got mad and put his hands on me again. He was following me around the house putting his hands on me and threw me down to the ground. He took my dining room set and threw it. My glass dishes shattered everywhere. My apartment was destroyed and my hand was bruised and bleeding. I called the cops and had him removed. A couple of weeks later, I received several of his text messages about how much he was hurting, how much he loved us and how sorry he was, and I found out what I needed to. He had left one of his old phones behind and I got into the phone. As if my heart had not been torn out enough. I found several videos, text messages, and messages in his social media, dating apps where he had been seeing over 20 girls, including two ex-girlfriends.

I was hurt and embarrassed when he was gone. I was ashamed. My heart was broken. But it was my own fault. Nobody can do to us what we don't allow. So I had to shift my focus to God, the root of my issues and why I would allow someone to do that to me, in front of my children. I had to begin to go through the process of healing, deliverance, and the worst part, feeling the built-up pain I had been suppressing all the years of my life, without numbing it with people and things of this world. I had to do the necessary work for change.

WARNINGS

- Pay close attention to your dreams. God always gives a warning before destruction (Proverbs 16:18).
- Listen to your inner guide, the Holy Spirit. He will never lie to you. Just because you don't know all the details, doesn't mean you're not on the right path.
- Confusion instead of peace. God is not the author of confusion.
- Not being in your Word
- Not praying
- Being too comfortable and not on alert
- Not asking the necessary questions from the beginning
- Not requiring a man to show you consistent effort

- Chasing versus being pursued
- Afraid to let go
- Fear
- Things aren't going right. God will allow everything to fall apart to get your attention
- Leaning on your own understanding
- Not asking God if this is the person for you, and waiting for confirmation
- Don't fall for potential
- Unequally yoked
- Neither of you are healed and delivered from childhood and past relationship trauma
- Fornicating
- Old habits start coming back up
- Can't sleep, lack of sleep and productivity in the assignments God has giving you
- Unable to fulfill your God-given assignments
- Isolation
- Attending church less
- Spending less time with God and idolizing this person and the relationship

LESSONS LEARNED

- Get healed and delivered from your past
- Get in your Word and spend time with God until He is all you need
- Pursue the assignments God has given you for your life
- Learn to love you first

- Learn to enjoy spending time alone with yourself so that you won't depend on anyone other than God to fill you
- Pursue God, not the things of this world
- Do the work necessary for change
- Invite God into your intricate parts of your being
- Deny self & surrender to God

CHAPTER 20

Gun Violence

BY KIMBERLY MOSES

I used to rob men when I was an exotic dancer. I started stripping at the age of thirteen. My friend and I would go to house parties and dance seductively. As we did that, men would throw money at us. We went from dancing clothed to just thongs. We made quick money often. Sometimes we would strip on the weekends at men's homes. Other times, it would be on a school night. We would meet these men in the night clubs, malls, or restaurants. We then set up a date and hustled them out of their cash. I was a slick talker and I knew the effect of alcohol. I realized that if I waited until a man got drunk or was slightly impaired, he would give me all or most of the money in his wallet.

Since we were underage, we couldn't legally strip in the clubs. So, we stripped at any home that we could find. One day, I had just bought myself a new car. The first car that I made by braiding hair all summer when I was 15 needed a new engine. I had just put a new transmission in it a few months earlier and I decided that it wasn't worth it. So, I got a white Nissan Sentra. I had a lot of cash from dancing, so I got a sound system installed and rims. One day I was driving blasting my sound system and a police officer came out of nowhere. I can still envision those blue flashing lights behind me. I was pulled over in a nice neighborhood. He wrote me a citation and I had to pay around $300 within a week.

I knew that I couldn't pay this in that time frame, so I called my friend. She said, "Don't worry. I'm talking to some guys and they want us to dance for them." She set it for the following day and when we finished, we walked out of the hotel room with more than what I needed. My friend and I outgrew the teenage club or parties. We weren't interested in boys our age because of their immaturity. We sought after grown men. My friend was bottom-heavy, and I was top-heavy, so we balanced each other out. If we went somewhere, the guys could choose which one of us they wanted. We were hustlers and we never got into a serious relationship with anyone. We just wanted their money and what they could do for us. If these men ever caught feelings, we would cut them off.

One night, my friend and I dressed up to go to an adult club. The owner of one of the biggest night clubs in the city was there. He was checking us out and pulled us over to the side while we stood in line. He let us into the building, and we bypassed everyone else that was waiting to get in. He took us to his office in the back of the building. He knew that we were underage, but he was cool with it. He wanted to date my friend, so they started a relationship. Through their relationship, we were treated like royalty. We sat in the VIP section and could get alcohol. We never had to wait in long lines, because we were the owner's girls.

One night, my friend planned to rob this man and I went along with it. He took us into his office while everyone else was partying upfront. We began to strip in front of him. She was blocking his view by kissing him and putting her breasts in his face. I was doing a lap dance from behind my friend. Since this man had his pants down around his ankles, I was able to get a big lump of money out of his pocket without him even noticing it. The money had a rubber band on it, and it was around 2,000 dollars. I quickly stuffed the money inside of my Nike Air Force Ones and pushed it to the top. My friend and I distracted the owner of the club by seducing him. He was mesmerized, and when we finished, we hurried out of the building before he could find out. Later, He tried to reach us but wasn't able too.

After we got away with this, I felt like I could rob guys easily. So, over the years, that's what I did. I would give them lap dancers and slide my hands in their pockets and pull out cash. They were too distracted or drunk to notice it. A couple of years went by and I met a new group of ladies. These ladies were tricks and had a pimp. He would set up appointments for them to have sex with men and they would pay him 25% of their earnings. I became friends with all of them and they tried to recruit me.

We would go dancing in different cities together, but afterward, they would go to hotels to make some extra money by doing tricks. They invited me to join in, but I would always decline because I made great money just by dancing and didn't want to sleep with random men. These women had no hustling skills, and they didn't know how to make men spend thousands on them like I did.

One day, we all went to a popular strip club out of town. The stage was a boxing ring, they had a grill inside, and the cooks made the best seafood. I would always order the shrimp. Most strips clubs didn't serve hot food, they only served peanuts at the bar. After we finished dancing, the women asked me to come along with them to do some tricks. That night was the first and the last time I agreed. We met a few guys in a ran down hotel nearby and the women started to perform sexual acts on them. Every part of the room was used. One man felt left out and he looked at me because I was standing up against the wall. So, he approached me, and I grabbed his hand and we went into the bathroom.

He gave me one hundred dollars to perform oral sex on him, but I couldn't do it. I felt sick and wanted to vomit because I was so turned off. I told him I couldn't, so he pulled out a gun then put it to my head. He cursed me out and demanded his money back. I was frightened and I gave it to him quickly. I rushed out of the bathroom and waited outside in my car for the women to finish. They each made around six hundred dollars. The next day, we all went to the mall and spent it on expensive outfits and food. When I was in my car, I thought to myself that I would never do tricks again. I was thankful that the man didn't pull the trigger.

Around this time, I got into a relationship with one of my customers and ended up falling hard for him. I had no idea that he was playing me and sleeping around. He later told me that he couldn't take me seriously because of my profession. He ended up giving me an STD called vaginitis, where I produced a fishy odor. I went to the doctor and received treatment. When I confronted him about it, he denied his cheating. So, I didn't ask him anymore about it but kept my eyes open. Once I made a pop-up visit and saw his ex-girlfriend pulling out of his yard. As soon as I got out of my car, he came outside to meet me and tried to explain what I'd seen. However, when I went inside, all the covers were off the bed, and he was washing them. Another time I picked up his phone and He yanked it out of my hands. He was really upset and ended our relationship. I thought his behavior was strange because I thought we were doing well. I was crushed. One day, a young lady called to inform me that she was pregnant by him and I was devastated. She knew all about me.

I called him about it because we were still dating even though we weren't officially together. He denied the whole thing and it infuriated me because I knew he was lying. I thought, "He must think I'm a fool. I'm not going to allow him to treat me like this." We met up later that week and we got into a huge argument outside of his house. I was enraged, so I picked up a metal rod in my car and bashed in the hood of his car. I wanted him to hurt like I was hurting. I knew the only way to break him was to destroy his car. He heard the noise and saw me beating his vehicle.

I hopped into my car and drove off. He chased me all around the city in his car. We were speeding dangerously through traffic. He cut a car off and pulled up right next to me. He rolled down his window and pulled out a pistol aiming it for my head. When I saw that, I ducked. I knew he was going to kill me, so I zoomed through oncoming traffic while running the red light. It was a miracle that I didn't get hit. Since it was a dangerous move, he couldn't follow me.

A couple of days later, after everything cooled off, we met up again to talk. However, we got into another fight. He punched me in the back of my head, and I ran out of his house. I jumped into my car to get away, but he was so angry. He picked up a big boulder in his yard and threw it straight into my windshield. Glass scattered everywhere, but the section in front of my face didn't break. I was an inch from death, but miraculously, the massive rock didn't touch me. It could've crushed my lungs and killed me. Glass could've gotten in my eyes blinding me or scratching my face. I drove up the street and I couldn't see anything out of the shattered glass. If someone was in the front seat with me, they would've gotten hit. I pulled around the corner and parked my car and called the police for help.

I knew that I was in a dark place and needed to stop what I was doing. However, I continued living this fast lifestyle for another few years before I got saved even though I was weary. Many women have been victims of gun violence and domestic abuse. They stay in dangerous relationships because they feel like sex can keep a man or change him. Only God can change that man. Others have died instantly when a boulder falls on their car. I remember driving through the Rocky Mountains and seeing "Watch out for Falling Rocks" signs everywhere. The first time I saw nets stapled alongside the mountains to catch the boulders from falling made my heart sink because it was breathtaking. I'm so blessed to be able to share my journey because if those men would've pulled the trigger, then I wouldn't be here today.

WARNING SIGNS

1. Sin equals death

Romans 6:23 says, "For the wages of sin is death; but the gift of God is eternal life through Jesus Christ our Lord."

I heard several preachers say, "Sin is like a credit card. You spend now and pay later." There is truth in that statement because the devil doesn't show you the consequences of your sin. So, you will end up paying the price later, such as getting infected with HIV, becoming pregnant, dying, your family destroyed, or jail time. Sin will put you on the path of destruction, which is a broad road, and a lot of people travel it (Matthew 7:13). I was on my way to hell and didn't realize it. I was being careless with my life and putting myself in harm's way. People will kill you if you rob them. Many people on the streets are murdered because they stole someone's drugs or took their money. Here I was, robbing men. Several men found out later that I took everything out of their pockets. They were looking for me, but I always laid low and made sure to avoid them. I was living a life of fear since I always had to look over my shoulders. What would've happened if these men were able to find me? They could've beaten, raped, and killed me.

LESSONS LEARNED

1. Love doesn't cheat or hit

Many people aren't knowledgeable about love. They feel like if they get hit on, cursed out, and mistreated, then that's love. They are deceived. Let's look at the following verses to see what love isn't.

1 Corinthians 13:4-6 (ESV) says, "Love is patient and kind; love does not envy or boast; it is not arrogant or rude. It does not insist on its own way; it is not irritable or resentful; it does not rejoice at wrongdoing but rejoices with the truth.

When someone loves you, then they will be patient with you. They will not be short-tempered and beat on you. They will not boast about things they have done for you while tearing your self-esteem down in the process. They will not cut you off all the time while you are speaking. They won't control you but listen to you so your emotional needs can be met. Your presence shouldn't irritate them, and you shouldn't feel like you have to walk on eggshells around them. They should enjoy your company and never keep a list of every wrong thing that you have ever done. I thought the men that I was in a relationship with loved me, but I discovered that he didn't. If someone loves you, they wouldn't sleep around on you endangering your health by infecting you with STDS. Many people stay in unhealthy relationships because there is something broken in them that only God can fix.

2. Only God can change someone

Many women have made the mistake of thinking that they can keep a man by sexing him up. What they fail to realize is he can get sex anywhere and lust prevents a man from being faithful. Lust can't be quenched or satisfied. They are going to want more of something. When that gets old, they are bored and onto the next person or power move. I used to feel that my looks could keep a man, but I was wrong. I thought that I was different and better than anyone this man ever dated. I tried to change him, but I was unsuccessful. If you are a child of God, give the Lord all your burdens and pray for your loved ones. In prayer, God will first show you your shortcomings because change begins with you. Every time I went to God and complained about someone, He showed me myself. "What about the time you lied, stole, cheated, etc?" I learned the hard way; your situation and people may not change, but you will as you spend time with God.

3. All money isn't good money

I was money hungry because I grew up poor. I liked the idea of getting fast cash and I would do anything to get it. I cheated, lied, robbed, betrayed others, and the list continues. I didn't realize that I was a child of darkness (1 Thessalonians 5:5) and destroying myself. The Bible warns us that the love of money is the root of all evil (1 Timothy 6:10). Many people have fallen away from the faith because of filthy lucre (1 Timothy 6:10). They lost their souls trying to gain worldly possessions (Matthew 16:26). Now, I realize that it's better to wait on God to provide then to compromise. I refuse to be like a dog returning to its vomit (Proverbs 26:11) by going back to my old lifestyle.

4. Know your worth

Many people stay in broken and toxic relationships because that's all they know. They don't feel like they deserve better, so they settle and remain stuck in dangerous circumstances. I felt like I had to show my body to get a man to notice me. When I saw other pretty women, I would try to outdo her by showing more skin. I felt good to turn more heads than her, but I didn't realize that I was attracting the wrong men. These men didn't want to marry me. They wanted to sleep with me and go on to the next female. I was blinded to the fact that men could never respect me because I didn't respect myself. No man wants to take a half-naked woman home to meet his mother. I went from one failed relationship to the next. It took getting saved and receiving deliverance that I realized I have a brain. I have a lot of great attributes other than beauty. Once, the Holy Spirit took me through a process of changing how I dressed, different types of men started to approach me. These men were godly and lived cleaned lives. They were the opposite of what I was used too. God still had to do further deliverance because I desired to date drug dealers even though I was saved. I stayed single for a while and focused on evangelism until the Lord told me that I was about to get married.

***

"357 MAGNUM"
BY JALONZO SAMUELS

In the summer of 1983, I looked down the barrel of a loaded 357 Magnum that was aimed to offer death to me once again. I am a transparent person and before I gave my life to the Lord, I smoked weed, drank alcohol, sold a little weed, hung out in the streets, the whole nine; not giving the enemy any glory, but just being honest. Let me tell you what happened. As I said, I sold a little weed. Well, this individual that I would purchase weight from fronted me a pound of marijuana. I got him to front me this package because on the last one I bought from him he didn't treat me right. So, I said that I would get him to front me this package to me and I just wasn't going to pay him, and I didn't.

A few weeks went by and one of his partners saw me. He told me that he wanted to see me. I told him to tell him that I will see him when I see him and that's that. As I stated, it was a summer day and I was sitting at a bar having a drink. Then this same guy walked in and sat beside me. We had a drink or two and some conversation. Suddenly he got up and walked out of the bar. I didn't think anything of it. I continued to do what I was doing, just chilling really. About thirty minutes had passed and I had decided to leave. But before I got up, this guy came back in and told me that the fellow that I had gotten the weed from was outside and wanted to see me. I was in no mood for drama, but I got up to see what was up.

When I got to his car and looked in to see what he wanted, I looked down the barrel of his 357. He asked me what was up. I told him nothing was up and that's when he pulled the trigger. Click. It didn't fire, but it was stuck, I was sure that I was shot. Click again. It didn't fire. He got out of the car, looked at the gun, pointed to the sky, pulled the trigger again and BOOM, the gun fired. He looked at me in disbelief and told me, "Just go! You owe me nothing! Just go!" God intervened again on my behalf, because he came to kill me, but the Lord caused the gun to misfire. I saw this guy ten years after this incident and he told me that he was now saved and is ministering the Gospel. It is all because of that incident because on that day, he knew that God was real because it was his plan to kill me. But it had to be God who saved me and stopped the bullet. Romans 8:28 states that God will cause all things to work together for our good because of love for Him and to them that a called according to His purpose. Death could not overtake me, because Life is His plan...

WARNING SIGNS

I already knew that I was playing with fire when I choose to take those goods from that brother. I heard in my spirit to not even confront this man about obtaining the goods that I got from him. I kept hearing, "No, leave that alone," but I thought that I could get away with it. God was warning me to stay away from death, but I overrode the voice and listened to the voice of the stranger.

LESSONS LEARNED

I learned that when we lean to our own understanding in the matters of life and do not heed to the voice of God pertaining to the direction that He has called us into, we open the doors for the enemy to bring total defeat and death to the plans and purposes of God for our lives. I came to the place to completely understand that, as Psalm 23 tells us, even though we may walk through the valley of the shadow of death, He Will prepare a table in the presence of our enemies. My table was the fact that He had anointed me for this present day to manifest His goodness and mercy, which followed me and caught up with me to give me victory over death and the plan of Satan.

CHAPTER 21

Lupus/Stroke

BY TIJUANA KILLIAN

At the age of sixteen, I began to have excruciating and unusual symptoms that consisted of a butterfly rash on my face, ulcers in my mouth, fever, fatigue, and joint pain everywhere. I couldn't move. My mom took me to the hospital to determine the problem because I was usually healthy. We were all scratching our heads in confusion. This turn of events wasn't at the most convenient time as my great grandmother had recently passed away. While we were grieving from a detrimental loss, I awaited my name to be called in the waiting room of the hospital. It was agonizing to sit in a chair, so I relieved myself by laying, rocking, and moaning on the floor.

Other patients with their families would enter the room and look at me. I could tell they were wondering, "Why is she on the floor?" I didn't care what they thought or what they said. Honestly, they were invisible to me. My mind was occupied with my condition.

After many tests and visits to the hospital, the doctors diagnosed me with systemic lupus erythematosus (SLE)[29], which is a chronic autoimmune condition. With this disorder, the immune system loses its ability to distinguish between a virus and healthy human tissue. As a result, the immune system attacks itself. This condition may create complications and further deteriorate the quality of life if left untreated.[30] Some people require anti-inflammatory drugs and chemotherapeutic agents to help treat the disease. It can affect the skin, joints, kidneys, brain, and other organs.[31]

In severe cases, it can lead to lupus cerebritis, a neuropsychiatric manifestation of SLE that presents clinically with confusion, lethargy, seizures, coma, mood changes, and even psychosis.[32] I developed lupus cerebritis years later.

After receiving the diagnosis, my family and I were further confused. We had never heard of this disease and didn't have a

---

29. "Systemic lupus erythematosus," Medline, Accessed February 28, 2020, https://medlineplus.gov/ency/article/000435.htm
30. "Systemic Lupus Erythematosus (SLE)," Healthline, Accessed February 28, 2020, https://www.healthline.com/health/systemic-lupus-erythematosus
31. "Lupus," Mayo Clinic, 2017, Accessed February 28, 2020, https://www.mayoclinic.org/diseases-conditions/lupus/symptoms-causes/syc-20365789
32. Patel, Rasna. "A Case of Lupus Cerebritis," Healio, 2018, Accessed February 28, 2020, https://www.healio.com/psychiatry/journals/psycann/2018-7-48-7/%7B9d542dd3-055b-4622-9e36-09039e204217%7D/a-case-of-lupus-cerebritiS

genetic history of it either. But at least we finally had a name for this mysterious illness. I was a sophomore in high school when I received the diagnosis. . High school was rough for me. Yes, I did have friends, special moments, lots of laughter, boyfriends, and I was on an amazing cheerleading squad. These memories were great, but the lupus was not going to be silenced.

During those years of high school, the suffering and discomfort of lupus were evident. The pain was agonizing, and I had extreme fatigue at times. Only a couple of people at my school knew what was occurring. There were many days that I felt secluded, misunderstood, and ugly. The doctors treated me with a medication called prednisone, which is an anti-inflammatory or an immunosuppressant.

Prednisone was bittersweet for me. On one hand, it was a means used to calm down an aggressive disease that was quickly attacking my body. On the other hand, I experienced dizziness, fluid retention, nausea, heartburn, mood changes, increased thirst, moon face, and weight gain in places I didn't want. My face, neck, and stomach were puffy. My whole upper torso reminded me of a football player. I hated it.

Moon face and weight gain sucked as a teenager, but it didn't compare to losing one of my high school friends to lupus. She and I got diagnosed with lupus the same year. I remember her moon face, hair loss, and weight gain as well. There were times she would be absent for days. Just like myself, she dealt with the situation privately and didn't stir up a lot of attention on herself or her circumstances. The times I saw her, she smiled, and we would talk. Our moments were normal and pleasant. I had no idea those memories would be the last we would share. After graduating high school, she died that summer at the age of 18. Along with her family, the whole school was shocked and devastated. I was at a loss for words. She was my friend for years before we entered high school.

So many emotions of disbelief, grief, and thankfulness hit my family and I. I was the same age as my friend. That could have been me. I was no different from her. We shared the same symptoms. Yet God allowed me to stay on earth longer. Thank you, Jesus.

Although Jesus Christ protected me and kept me all those years with lupus, the devil was trying his hardest to kill me and my destiny. In the years going forth, I've had life threatening lupus related complications during childbirth. I lost two babies. Remember, lupus is a disease that attacks the body, organs, and tissue. It attacked my fetuses. It also struck my kidneys, heart, and brain (stroke).

When I first heard, I survived cerebellar infarct or (cerebellar stroke). I was shocked. My thoughts were, "Are you kidding me, so you really tried to take me up out of here, huh devil?" It was pretty bad to the extent of memory loss.

In April of 2007, I lived with a friend and her family. She was older than me and assisted in my spiritual development. "You were fighting for your life for three days," she recounts. The warfare started after I received the baptism of the Holy

Spirit with evidence of speaking in tongues. I desired the gift of tongues for years after I got saved. I sought the Lord for this gift. Suddenly alone in my friend's daughter's room , the tongues came. I believe I spoke in every native language that day. I know now that I needed my spiritual language for the turn of events to come. The devil had tried to kill me.

According to my friend, I was in and out of tongues for three days straight, which wasn't my normal prayer. My movements and the sounds coming out of my mouth were different. I was battling. I was in warfare. For three days, I didn't sleep. I got no physical rest. She would hear me praying at night and would ask God to cover me. I didn't eat anything either. I supernaturally fasted for three days and didn't realize I was fasting.

During those three days, I felt lethargic and not myself. I would call for her son, who I considered to be my brother to help me to the bathroom. On the third day, I yelled out for assistance to the bathroom. While in the restroom, I collapsed before he could leave. He scooped me up and frantically called to his mom, "She needs to go to the hospital," while carrying me down the stairs.

I didn't know what was happening to me because I blacked out. At the hospital, I experienced fevers, chills, headache, nausea, vomiting, lethargy, confusion, and was in and out of consciousness. One moment, I was alert and I knew my surroundings. The next moment I was out instantly. I would wake up in different rooms wondering how I got there.

With the headache and other symptoms that I was having, they performed a brain MRI that discovered a cerebellar infarct. A cerebellar infarct (or cerebellar stroke) occurs when a blood vessel is blocked or bleeding, causing complete interruption to the portion of the cerebellum. The cerebellum is the portion of the brain that controls movement and maintains balance. Cerebellar stroke can cause mortality or permanent injury.5[33]

Along with a cerebellar stroke, my heart rate had dropped to dangerous levels. I was unconscious at this time. The doctors were running out of options. Some tests they ran came back normal. They didn't know what was making my heart rate drop. The lady I was living with at the time was in the hospital room with me. She recalls a younger doctor wanting to give me a medicine that's used to treat heart patients. He felt led to try this medicine. The doctor left my room to discuss his decision with the other team of doctors. They gave him the green light. As soon as he stuck the medicine through my chest, I sat up and said, "I'm reaping the harvest God promised me, take back what the devil stole from me," then laid back down. These are lyrics from the song "Faithful Is Our God," by Hezekiah Walker.

The doctor was shocked by my sudden reaction. I had been out for a while. I could barely hold up my body weight. My body was limp. The medicine worked and he told my loved ones to keep praying because it was working. I began to get better. I was treated for the stroke and soon afterward, I was discharged.

---

33. "Cerebellar Stroke," Healthline, Accessed February 28, 2020, https://www.healthline.com/health/cerebellar-stroke

WARNING SIGNS

1. Get Grief Counseling

I received Lupus symptoms after my great grandmother passed away. Maybe the symptoms started because of that turn of event in my life, or perhaps not. I believe it could have made my diagnosis easier to cope with if I had dealt with that first.

2. Go To The Hospital Sooner

- While living with my friend, I needed assistance to the bathroom for multiple days. That wasn't normal behavior for me.
- During that same time at her house, I was lethargic and weak.

LESSONS LEARNED

1. You're Not Going Anywhere Until It's Your Time

My friend and I from high school were the same age and got diagnosed with lupus the same year. The Lord kept me here longer for His plan and purpose for my life. There is a time for everything, and everything on earth has its special season. There is a time to be born and a time to die.- Ecclesiastes 3:1-2

2. Healthier Eating

Throughout the years and even more recently, God has been giving me healthier food options. I have been told to eat hummus, more protein, and to consume lemon water. The inflammation in my body is linked to lupus, so I must digest anti-inflammatory foods. This hasn't been an easy transition, because I am used to eating anything I want. Nevertheless, I am enjoying my new healthier lifestyle. I feel better, as well!

3. God Is Faithful

I was having symptoms of a stroke before I got to the hospital, and God shielded me from unknown danger. While in the hospital, I was in and out of consciousness and God was with me. I will never leave you, nor forsake you.- Hebrews 13:5

CHAPTER 22

Nightmare Spirits

BY STEPHANIE HAM

It began when I was about 12 or 13 years old when the devil tried to kill me in my sleep. I used to live in the pink house owned by the housing authority in East New York, Brooklyn. That's where I encountered a lot of my warfare. Since my mother was not saved during my childhood, it was difficult to explain to her what I was battling. As a result, I had to experience these things without much support.

I never like the movie "Poltergeist" or the "Exorcist" because I had enough strange things to happen to me. I felt like there was always some dark cloud following me. I saw people die around me and I never wanted to go to sleep. I used to hate sleeping in the dark because I would hear and see things, so I would sleep with the cover over my head, hoping that it would all go away. One morning I was home alone, and it was if something was choking me and I couldn't breathe or able to wake up. Something demonic was holding me down on the bed, trying to kill me. I tried falling off the bed, but nothing happened. I tried calling out to my mother for help but remembered that no one was home. Then the words of my great grandmother, Lizzy Darby, played in my mind, "Whenever you're in trouble just call on the name of Jesus." I was desperate! I thought, "If I die, then my mother would never know that it was the devil who had killed me." As I laid helplessly with no strength left in my body, I whispered, "Jesus, Jesus, Jesus." Suddenly that demonic spirit was gone. I fell to my knees in relief that it had set me free. That mean old devil had it out for me and I never knew why.

WARNING SIGNS

I had the spirit of fear upon me which opened up the door to nightmare spirits.

LESSONS LEARNED

1. Call On the Name of Jesus.

I learned to call on the name of Jesus when I face a demonic attack. The greatest power to fight against the forces of darkness is Jesus. Jesus gives us the power and ability to fight against the devil. The Scripture says that those who call upon the name of Lord shall be saved. You have to know that Jesus will protect you. No matter what dark times you are going through, if you just pray and seek Him, He will answer your prayer according to His will and loving, and kindness. He will make a way for you to escape the traps of death and the devices of the enemy.

CHAPTER 23

Pulmonary Embolism

BY STEPHANIE HAM

It was June 20, 2018, around 8 a.m. I woke up to my grandbaby Kelsey saying, "Good morning Nana." As I sat up in the chair, I gave her a big hug, then reached for the remote to watch cartoons with her. I was feeling just fine, but suddenly I rolled off of the couch and passed out, hitting my head on the floor. My grandchild's mother turned me on my back and performed CPR. She called the ambulance, and someone tapped me as they took my vital signs. "Are you okay?" I looked around, trying to figure out what had happened. My breathing was very shallow. I was out for a long. As they helped me to the bathroom, they got me ready to be put on the stretcher. They took me to Richmond University Hospital in Staten Island, New York. The doctors examined me and ran different types of tests, such as MRIs and

X-rays. They discovered that I had pulmonary embolisms or blood clots in my heart and lungs. As a team of doctors came to the room, they said how lucky I was to survive such an attack because most people don't make it. The body begins to shut down. God used my doctor to bring me back to life.

WARNING SIGNS

I had previous medical issues. We must be on top of our health.

LESSONS LEARNED

1. I am highly favored and loved by God.

He has my best interest at heart. He loves me enough to allow me to live and come back to write this book so that His people will not go to hell and burn in the lake of fire.

CHAPTER 24

Deadly Snakes

BY STEPHANIE HAM

I was living at 327 Fletcher Street in Bennettsville, South Carolina, and working at a plant in Marlboro County. My boys, Yahdiah and Obadiah, had a doctor's appointment, so I kept them home from school. On any other day, we normally have a movie night and all sleep in the living room. But for some reason, I heard the Holy Spirit say, "No. Tell them to go sleep in their own beds tonight." So, I obeyed then around 6 a.m. I got up, as I usually did, to iron our clothes. I noticed that there was an extra cord next to the outlet was located. However, it wasn't a cord but a diamond head baby rattlesnake that was all curled up next to the iron. I thank God that when I plugged the iron in, the snake did not attack and bite me because it would have been fatal. But to God be the glory, I was able to get my two small children out of the house. We ran to the neighbor's house to call 911.

When the dispatcher asked, "What is your emergency? How may we help you?" I told them what had happened. They then said that they would send the police right away. As soon as the police arrived, they looked for the snake. They said, "Oh. We don't see any snakes." When I pointed to the snake to show them where it was, one of the officers came into the house. The Caucasian police officer stated that if he cannot shoot it, then he doesn't need to be there. So, he walked out of the apartment. As Office Miller followed his partner to their swat car, he stated that I needed to call the animal patrol. I was surprised to see such muscular officers running quickly to get away from a tiny snake. We sat outside and waited for the animal patrol to arrive. When they arrived, they caught the snake by pulling it outside, then cutting its head off.

It was nothing but the grace of God who kept my family protected. Had I been disobedient and did a movie night, my children and I would be dead and probably bitten by the snake.

WARNING SIGNS

The Holy Spirit warned and gave me instructions. If I were disobedient, then it could've cost me my life.

LESSONS LEARNED

1. Listen to the prompting of the Holy Spirit.

I am grateful that I had a prayer life and was listening to the Holy Spirit. He spared my children and I. We were protected by the grace of God.

CHAPTER 25

Suicide

BY KIMBERLY MOSES

Many people have ended their lives prematurely by committing suicide. It's shocking to see pastors, leaders, and our favorite celebrities go this route. "I thought they were happy. They seemed to have everything going for themselves. I didn't recognize any warning signs that they were suicidal." These are some of the things that I have heard people say when someone kills themselves. A person can appear to be okay on the outside, but inside there is a war with demonic forces. Satan is an influencer because he can't take over our free will unless we allow him to do so. He makes suggestions and plants evil seeds in our minds. If someone isn't praying, spending time with God, meditating on the Word, fasting, and casting those thoughts down, then they may feel like suicide is the only way out. That is far from the truth.

Killing ourselves doesn't solve anything. The pain is only temporal, and Jesus promises us peace to deal with the trials in life.

2 Corinthians 4:17 (ESV) says, "For this light momentary affliction is preparing for us an eternal weight of glory beyond all comparison."

John 16:33 (ESV) says, "I have said these things to you, that in me you may have peace. In the world, you will have tribulation. But take heart; I have overcome the world."

We aren't alone in our valley seasons (Psalms 24:3). The enemy wants us to lose all hope and give up, so our destinies are forfeited. He is on a mission overtime to kill, steal, and destroy (John 10:10). He knows that you are a threat to his kingdom when you are fully walking in your God-given purpose. Life is a gift and when the spirit of suicidal is present, a person despises the gift. We must be careful about what we watch or listen to on television, radio, social media, and from the people around us. We don't want to be persuaded in any fashion that suicide is the answer. When someone prematurely ends their life, they are hurting their loved ones. They can't see how selfish their actions are when this path is taken. God needs you and so do others who love you. Don't listen to the devil when he tells you that no one cares about you. God loves you so much that He sent Jesus to die on the cross for you (John 3:16).

I first started feeling suicidal when I was going through marital strife with my ex-husband. I was controlling and couldn't handle the fact that my life was spiraling out of control. I had to oversee every detail of my family and how things played out. When my ex-husband wanted out of the marriage, I gave him an ultimatum. "If you leave me, then I'll kill myself." It seemed to work the first few times, but things went from bad to worse. The domestic violence, cheating, and the lies were too much. The marriage was toxic and threatening to commit suicide allowed the devil to play in my mind.

I was in a dark place and wanted to be set free. I was suffering from anxiety and the devil was speaking to me all the time. "I hate you. Why don't you just kill yourself for real? You are worthless. No one will ever love you. You are so stupid. You aren't pretty enough, that's why he cheated. If you don't kill yourself, then I am going to kill you." The devil told me several things like this throughout the day. I would yell at him, "Shut up!" Sometimes, I grabbed my temples or my ears, trying to silence him because I was frustrated. I didn't know how to fight, but I knew that God could help me get free.

One day, I took a paring knife out of the drawer in the kitchen and held out my forearm. I began to cut, but the knife was dull and left a few scratches. I was even more irritated that I failed at cutting myself, I said to myself, "What am I doing? I can't kill myself." Another time, I was driving in my city, and the enemy spoke to me. "Why don't you drive your car into the lake at the park." I felt an urge come upon me to do it, but I could tell that the Lord was also working because I had been praying for help. As soon as the unction came, it left. Weeks went by, and so many demonic suggestions were tormenting my mind on how to commit suicide: overdose, fire, jumping off a building, drowning, and the list continues.

One day, my ex-husband and I got into a big fight, so I left to go to church while he stayed home. I just needed God to set me free from the demons that were harassing me. In the middle of the service, I heard the devil tell me to go outside. I got up out of my seat and grabbed my purse. It was like I was a zombie. I walked out the door and I saw my ex-husband driving out of the parking lot, which infuriated me. He didn't want to come to church and lied that he was coming. I was enraged and stormed to my truck. I got inside and I drove recklessly through the parking lot of the church. My ex-husband was parked at the light waiting for it to turn green. I was approaching him, and my foot slammed on the accelerator. I could hear the sound of speed. The next thing I know, I am ramming his car. It was surreal and I blacked out for a second. I snapped! It was like I was being controlled and an angry person came into my body. A few seconds later, I was in my right mind, and fear came over me. "What have I done. Oh no. I must flee!" There were a few onlookers and they were shocked. I heard someone yell, "Stop! Enough!" So, I sped down the road. My ex-husband wasn't hurt. However, I caused about $2500 worth of damages that I later paid in restitution.

I drove back to our home and was so afraid that I packed some bags. I was about to flee across the country, but suddenly the police came knocking on my door. I tried to hide at first, but I just surrendered. I was arrested and placed in the suicide ward. I remember that I had to stay in my cell for 23 hours and I could only come out for one hour each day. Sixty minutes went by so fast because I had to shower, choose a book to read and make a phone call. I had to wear a dark green Velcro vest and wasn't allowed to wear any undergarments because they were preventing me from using a bra or underwear to hang myself. The regular prisoners wore dark grey scrubs. They had more freedom than those in the suicide ward. My cell had a mirror, a toilet, a desk, and a bunk bed. I wasn't allowed to have a pillow but could have one thin small blanket. I couldn't keep a toothbrush, comb, or any hygiene products in the cell. When it was time to shower, the guard handed those things to me along with a towel, soap, and lotion. I was becoming claustrophobic from the confinement.

A therapist came by to questioned me. "Kimberly, on a scale from 1 to 10, what is your will to live?" I replied sarcastically, "A zero." She said, "That's not an option." She told me that she would be back to check on me because she had to complete her assessment on my mental status. I had a lot of time to think. At first, I had the spirit of murder on me. I thought about different ways to kill my ex-husband. I hated him for all the things he put me through, and I wanted him to suffer. When it was the 24th hour, the guard let me out of my cell. I showered and made my phone calls. My time was running out and I knew that I had to go back into the cell soon. I wasn't allowed to bring a puzzle or game with me but could bring a book. I looked on the shelf and saw many options. I was drawn to this dark green book that matched the vest I had on. I picked it up. It was called, *"Doing His Time: Meditations and Prayers for Men and Women in Prison,"* by James C. Vogelzang and Lynn Vanderzalm.

I went back into my cell and started to read. Every page that I turned, I sensed a feeling that I hadn't felt in years. I was feeling peace and the presence of God. Tears began to fall as I was reminded of God's mercy and grace. "You mean to tell me that God still loves and cares about me after all of this? I messed up! I'm going through a divorce! My life is over. What good do I have to offer?" These were some of my thoughts. I read a few more chapters and paused because it was on forgiveness. "Lord, I am so sorry for turning my back on You and ignoring Your voice. I heard You gently speaking to me, telling me to walk away many times, but I was so angry. I ignored you! I kept fighting and arguing. Please forgive me. I want You to give me another chance. I promise to live right."

I cried as the peace of God came upon me. I felt so refreshed and pure inside. The spirit of murder left me. I realized that I didn't want my ex-husband to die because I still cared for him. I didn't know what life had in store for me, but I knew that I had found God in my jail cell. I continued to read and became hopeful. Burdens that I was carrying for months were supernaturally lifted.

The next day, the therapist returned to do a follow-up assessment. She asked me the same question. "Kimberly, on a scale from 1 to 10, what is your will to live?" I replied, "An eleven." Her eyes widened, and she asked, "What changed." "Well, I am reading this book and I realize that I have my children to live for. I don't want to be selfish. They need me," I said. "Good for you. I'm glad to hear that. You are absolutely right," she said as she walked away, jotting down some notes. Shortly after, I stood before the judge to receive my sentence. My sister and her husband drove thirteen hours to bail me out of jail then they turned back around because they had to be at work. I didn't get a chance to see them because being processed out of jail takes some time. I remember walking out of the jail and getting into my truck. I had nowhere to go because my ex-husband put a restraining order on me, and I couldn't go back to the home we shared. I only had sixty-five dollars in my account, which was enough to get a hotel for the night. I needed to think about my next moves. I was in the worst trial of my life but was happy to know that God was now with me.

WARNING SIGNS

1. Countenance Change

When someone is battling suicide, look for any changes in their behavior. Are they putting up a front or pretending to be something that they are not? Some people who are suicidal may overly act like they are happy, and everything is okay. Pay attention to the red flags and asked the Holy Spirit questions. "Lord, show me what this person is dealing with, so I can know how to pray for them. Give me wisdom to minister to them." With other people, the warning signs can be more obvious. You know they are depressed because they want to sleep their life away or make the room dark. They might try to avoid others and withdraw.

A couple of months after I got out of jail, I was dealing with suicidal thoughts again. The Lord had given me a list of 21 books to write. I had written my first book but couldn't focus on writing the second book. I laid on my couch for three days. I only got up to use the bathroom. I didn't eat nor shower. I avoided everyone's phone calls. My family and friends were very concerned about me. My house was very dark, with minimum light shining through. I tried to sleep my life away. I prayed, "Lord, I want to die. I don't want to live anymore because the pain that I'm feeling is unbearable." At that moment, the Lord spoke to me, "It's not your time to die yet. You have work to do." When I heard His voice, the layers of heaviness left, and I jumped up. I showered and ate. Remember, people that are closest to you know that something is wrong. Let the Lord change your countenance with His glory so you can radiate His presence.

Numbers 6:24-26 (ESV) says, "The Lord bless you and keep you; the Lord make his face to shine upon you and be gracious to you; the Lord lift up his countenance[a] upon you and give you peace."

LESSONS LEARNED

1. God loves you

The devil will tell you that the world is better off without you. That's not true. If you have nothing to live for, at least allow God to give you something. I wanted to kill myself because my ex-husband was an idol in my life. I thought that I had nothing to live for once he walked out of my life. I felt that no one would ever love me, which was far from the truth. God showed me how much He loves and cares about me. He feels the same about you. The Holy Spirit is our comforter. I remember feeling the pains of divorce and still having to see my ex-husband sometimes when we would exchange the children. The fire of God would come upon me and this warming sensation would go down my arms. I know that was a reminder that I wasn't alone. If people let you down, there is still a loving God with His arms stretched wide, waiting to shower you in His compassion and mercy.

2. There is hope

I felt like there was no hope for me and that my life was over. Romans 5:3-4 says, "And not only so, but we glory in tribulations also: knowing that tribulation worketh patience; And patience, experience; and experience, hope."

I didn't realize that the end of a thing is the beginning of something else (Ecclesiastes 7:8). There is life after divorce, heartache, pain, and loss. The sun will shine again, and you will get stronger. God took the shameful things and used them for His glory. He set me free of others' opinions, so now I'm able to tell my story fully. God blessed me in front of the people who counted me out and who said I would never make it. When I decided to live, He anointed me and began to use me in signs, wonders, and miracles. If you stumble, get back up again. Keep trying. Jesus is the source of our hope. He wants us to win.

Jeremiah 29:11 (ESV) says, "For I know the plans I have for you, declares the Lord, plans for welfare[a] and not for evil, to give you a future and a hope."

3. Cast down thoughts

When the enemy whisper lies, we must cast them down immediately.

2 Corinthians 10:5 says, "Casting down imaginations, and every high thing that exalteth itself against the knowledge of God, and bringing into captivity every thought to the obedience of Christ."

We have to find a scripture to stand on as a weapon. We must meditate to get the Word of God into our hearts. I remember when I first started to meditate on the Word. I would think about it then speak it repeatedly. I began to fast because some things don't come out except by prayer and fasting (Matthew 17:21). When I started to do these things, the tormenting spirits in my mind become uncomfortable. They would scream, curse me out, and beg for me to stop doing what I was doing. They would lie and say what I was doing would never work. I knew that the Word of God is true (John 17:17), so I ignored them by resisting them. Eventually, the devil left, and the Holy Spirit began to do His will in my life.

4. Suicide is never the answer

Suicide doesn't solve anything. It's a cowardly thing to do. You will go to hell for playing God and ending your life. Suicide is a sin and those who sin will not inherit the Kingdom of God (Revelation 22:15; 1 Corinthians 6:9–10; Galatians 5:19–21; Ephesians 5:5; 1 Timothy 1:9; Hebrews 12:14).

We must face our challenges because growth and wisdom are gained in the process. We are overcomers in Jesus Christ and walk in victory. When I was depressed during the holidays, the Lord gave me the strength to get out of bed and enjoy my day. He will do the same for you. Don't allow people to steal your joy, peace, and happiness. The best is yet to come. Suicide is a permanent solution to a temporary problem. You are only given one life to live and once your life is over in this world, you can't come back. God allows us to go through certain challenges to birth greater things within. You will make it. Thus far, I have authored over twenty books because of my trials. These books are blessing lives and making an impact for the Glory of God. Imagine the good that will come out of your life if you decide to stick around and live.

***

TEENAGE PREGNANCY

BY ALLENA DOUGLAS

When I look back over my life, I praise God continually for His Grace and Mercy. There are numerous accounts of where I almost died. At the age of five years old, I can recall spending an afternoon with my uncle. He was very endearing and always doted on my sister and I. On this particular day he had a visitor. I can remember a brief conversation between the two and the man left in a hurry. My uncle didn't say anything else. He sat on the couch quietly. Unbeknownst to me, he had been assassinated. The killer allowed me to live. I don't remember much from that day, but I thank God for shielding and protecting me.

I grew up as a young lady that had a passion to know God. We attended our home church, where I sang in the choir, and participated in multiple programs. I played basketball in high school and really did great. I was always encouraged and told that I would do well in life. God placed women and family in my life to speak positive words. My life took a turn when I became pregnant. My family was called and told that I could no longer be in the choir or do anything in the church because I was an unwed mother. I was devastated. Everywhere I went, there was a negative stigmatism. I had words spoken, such as "I would never be anything. I would never get married because I was spoiled." My self-esteem was low, and I was heartbroken because I thought God didn't love me.

One day, my teacher Mrs. Thelma Williams called me in after class. She said, "God said you will live and not die. Forget about the negative talk that the other kids are saying. You are beautiful, smart, brave, and courageous. John 8:7 says that He that is without sin cast the first stone. Your child is a blessing from God. You work after school; you are a well-known basketball player and you are a good girl. Hold your head up." I cried a cleansing cry. I knew I was going to be ok.

She said one more scripture: Jeremiah 29:11, "For I know the plans that I have for you. Declares the Lord plans to prosper you and not to harm you. Plans to give you hope and a future." Because of the negativity, I was thinking of ending my life. I thank God for my mother, grandparents, siblings, family and friends that prayed for me. They didn't allow me to give up. I love my children. They grew up to be awesome men and a woman of God. I could have died but God had a plan.

WARNING SIGNS

- My mother always told us not to let anyone in the house while she was at work.
- I disobeyed my mother.
- The boy was more mature than I was.
- His friends were older, and they were always partying.

LESSONS LEARNED

- I learned that despite my sin, God loves my child and me.
- Always be prayerful and make sure the voice you hear is God's.
- Be careful of the negative words you speak over people. The power of life and death are in the tongue.
- Suicide is real. I could have been a statistic, but God had a plan.
- I discovered the National Suicide Hotline. It is a great resource.

About The Authors

Kimberly Moses started off her ministry as Kimberly Hargraves. She is highly sought after as a prophetic voice, intercessor and prolific author. There is no doubt that she has a global mandate on her life to serve the nations of the world by spreading the Gospel of Jesus Christ. She has a quickly expanding worldwide healing and deliverance ministry. Kimberly Moses wears many hats to fulfill the call God has placed on her life as an entrepreneur over several businesses including her own personal brand Rejoice Essentials which promotes the Gospel of Jesus Christ.

She also serves as a life coach and mentor tomany women. She is also the loving mother of two wonderful children. She is married to Tron. Kimberly has dedicated her life to the work of ministry and to serve others under the call God has placed over her life. Kimberly currently resides in South Carolina.

She is a very anointed woman of God who signs, miracles and wonders follow. The miraculous and incessant testimonies attributed to her ministry are incalculable, with many reporting physical and mental healing, financial breakthroughs, debt cancellations and other favorable outcomes. She is known across the globe as a servant who truly labors on behalf of God's people through intercession.

She is the author of The Following:

"Overcoming Difficult Life Experiences with Scriptures and Prayers"
"Overcoming Emotions with Prayers"
"Daily Prayers That Bring Changes"
"In Right Standing,"
"Obedience Is Key,"
"Prayers That Break The Yoke Of The Enemy: A Book Of Declarations,"
"Prayers That Demolish Demonic Strongholds: A Book Of Declarations,"
"Work Smarter. Not Harder. A Book Of Declarations For The Workforce,"
"Set The Captives Free: A Book Of Deliverance."
"Pray More Challenge"
"Walk By Faith: A Daily Devotional"
"Empowering The New Me: Fifty Tips To Becoming A Godly Woman"
"School of the Prophets: A Curriculum For Success"
"8 Keys To Accessing The Supernatural"
"Conquering The Mind: A Daily Devotional"

"Enhancing The Prophetic In You"
"The ABCs of The Prophetic: Prophetic Characteristics"
"Wisdom Is The Principal Thing: A Daily Devotional"
"It Cost Me Everything"
"The Making Of A Prophet: Women Walking in Prophetic Destiny"
"The Art of Meditation: A Daily Devotional"
"Warfare Strategies: Biblical Weapons"
"Becoming A Better You"

You can find more about Kimberly at
www.kimberlyhargraves.com

For Rejoice Essential Magazine
www.rejoiceessential.com

For Beauty Products
www.rejoicingbeauty.com

Please write a review for my books on Amazon.com

Support this ministry:
Cashapp: $ProphetessKim
Paypal.me/remag

Joseph A. Samuels was born in Philadelphia, PA. He is an author, prophetic minister, musician, elder, and is an active member at the Greater Faith International Ministries in Varnville, South Carolina, as well as the Everlasting Gospel Kingdom Ministries in Columbia, South Carolina. Joseph has an anointing to teach and preach the Word of God, which has taken him to various cities, states, and countries. He presently operates a blog entitled Kingdom Principles, which teaches the structural foundations of the Kingdom of God and the exposition revelations regarding the Father's seasonal directions for the Body of Christ. He and his wife, Yolanda, also operate a blog entitled Becoming One Flesh, which gives Biblical guidelines for married couples and for those assessing their future for marriage.

Joseph is an United States Army Veteran, where he served for nine years as a Medical Specialist. He has traveled to many countries during his military duties. He has a Bachelor's Degree in Business Management, which while in college, he enjoyed a great career playing college basketball. His college basketball career continued even into his service in the military, which afforded him to play for the All-Army Team to represent the United States all over the globe. Joseph has had a semi-professional basketball career, which afforded him to try out for several teams in the National Basketball Association (NBA).

Joseph has worked for the Department of Veteran's Affairs Hospital as a counselor for six (6) years and also as a Grief Counselor for various Funeral Homes and families through his business, "The Joseph Company."

He is a kind and compassionate person that will always lend a helping hand or a kind word to anyone that he meets. He has the heart of a servant and does not think that he is too great to get his hands dirty in the assistance of those that need his help.

Joseph is married to Yolanda Samuels, whom he cherishes and loves as Christ loves the church. He has two daughters, (Angela and Joy) and four grandchildren, (Terrell, Tierra, Taylor, and Nigel). He has endured many trials and victories in his life. God has used all of the ups and downs to point him in a direction to establish him as a mighty tool in the manifestation of the plan and purposes for the Kingdom. His life has become a testament to the goodness of God. He is forever evolving into the vessel of the goodness of God in every aspect of leadership in the Father's everlasting gospel to the nations.

Presently, many doors that had been closed to him are now opened to minister to the people of God and also to those that do not know of the Father's grace and mercy to those that believe in the finished work of Jesus Christ. He has now been called into the office of an Apostle in the Kingdom and considers it an honor to serve God's people and to not only be used but also to be usable in the Father's Plan.

Stephanie Ham is the founder and CEO of Misfits To The Nation, But Chosen By God's Creation. Before marriage, she was known as Stephanie Whack. She is a woman after God's own heart and an intercessor. Stephanie is married to Leo A. Ham. She is a mother of three sons, and four grandchildren: two boys and two girls. She happens to be the #1 Best Seller Book Writing Scribe for The Kingdom. When God called her, He said, "I must work the works of him that sent me, while it is day: the night cometh, when no man can work. As long as I am in the world, I am the light of the world {John 9:4-5}."

Stephanie's favorite Scripture is: "For I know the thoughts that I think toward you, saith the Lord, thoughts of peace, and not of evil, to give you an expected end" (Jeremiah 29:11).

Stephanie's ministry is all about encouraging, uplifting the brokenhearted, hurting, and abused men and women of God. When you're broken from the inside, it's hard to believe in a God who you cannot see. You don't know how He can possibly love someone you... Right? I had to learn that God's Word concerning our lives means so much to Him that He died to save us. Amen. It does not matter to Our Savior if we are a misfit. But what does concerns Him is that we are the core of Jesus's very being. Know that we're Misfits with A Purpose that can change the Nation. God has given Stephanie a keen discernment, intelligence, and a passion for prayer. She loves seeing souls saved. It doesn't matter if you're called an outcast. God loves you. God died for you to live and have life more abundantly.

She has attended the following churches along her Journey:

- St. Michael's Hope Ministry: Apostle Michael, Prophetess Sharon Woodham CLIO, SC.
- Word Of Life Pastor Hodges Bennettsville SC, Solid Rock Holiness: Apostle Ervin Dease and First Lady Mary Dease "aka Spiritual Parents' Bennettsville, SC.
- New Creation Christian Church: Bishop Wesley V. Knight & Prophetess Adrian Knight "aka Spiritual Parents" Brooklyn, NY.
- The Doors Of Hope: Bishop Michael Blue& First Lady Melinda Blue from Marin SC.
- Her educational background consists of the following:
- Word Of Life Bible College Studied: The book of Revelation, The Tabernacle, Homiletics. 2002, In Bennettsville SC.
- Undergraduate Nyack College study General, Counseling, Abnormal and Child Psychology. Old, New Testament, etc. 2010- 2013

In Manhattan, NY, God started dealing with Stephanie's life and how she felt about herself. She received the vision for her ministry between 2011- 2012 and birthed it out in 2020.

God placed her around people who believed in her and what she couldn't see in herself. God was in the midst the whole time. Nevertheless, everything happens in God's timing.

BIOGRAPHY - EMELIA ADJEI

Emelia Adjei is a philanthropist and author of two books titled – "Accelerate to Glory" & "Life in the Diaspora." She's a Christian, Kingdom-minded and passionate about spreading the goodness and greatness of God. She emigrated from her motherland country of Ghana –West Africa to the USA with nothing but dreams of a better life. She overcame many challenges, including near homelessness but stayed determined, focused, and worked hard to pursue her dreams. She has a Master's Degree in Business Administration. Emelia's been featured in a documentary movie and magazines.

Emelia is driven, authentic, and down to earth. She's constantly reinventing herself and setting new goals. She's about purpose and living a fulfilled life. She's committed to using her life experiences to empower and inspire others to pursue their dreams and reach their full potential. By drawing from her personal and professional experiences, Emelia uses practical principles and strategies to mentor people to break through barriers that stop them from making their dreams become a reality.

She's compassionate and has a big heart of giving and helping the poor and needy. She runs a non-profit organization called "Empower The Children – ETC" that supports orphans and less privileged children in Africa. ETC provides free food, clothing and toiletries to low-income communities. The foundation serves the youth through free education and resources to broaden their knowledge and perspective on life to become good productive citizens. The organization also donates books to schools and medical supplies to hospitals and clinics.

One of her favorite quotes is "I alone cannot change the world, but I can cast a stone across the waters to create many ripples," by Mother Teresa.

Her hobbies are writing, reading, organizing, and enjoying the outdoors. She is a girly girl who enjoys shopping and make-up. She appreciates the simple and thoughtful things in life. Emelia is funny and doesn't take herself so seriously. She has a sweet tooth and will choose dessert over any meal.

Emelia resides in U.S.A with her family. She's thankful and humbled by the opportunities God has blessed her. Her mission is to inspire, transform lives, and make a difference in diverse ways.

www.EmeliaAdjei.com
www.EmpowerTheChildren.org

Michelle Loatman is a prophetic voice, an intercessor with a servant's heart, striving to cultivate her spiritual gifts and ministerial anointing, to effect change in the lives of others, for the glory of God, and the enhancement of His Kingdom. She was born in Bridgeton, New Jersey, on April 17, 1978. Michelle is the middle of three children. As a child, she attended West Park United Methodist Church of Shiloh, New Jersey. Michelle received her education in the Bridgeton Public School System. However, she graduated high school from Nikos Academy for Girls in Williamstown, New Jersey, on June 10, 1995. Michelle received Jesus as her personal Lord and Savior at the age of 15, at Gloucester County Christian Church, under Pastor Bruce J. Sofia. She was baptized in the Holy Spirit at the age of 16, on August 19, 1995, at Church of Christ in Pitman, New Jersey. Michelle accepted the calling on her life of ministry at the age of 41 years old. Michelle is a member of Word Alive Worship Center, under Pastors Anthony Bailey and Pastor Glenda Bailey, where she has also received her diaconate and ministerial training.

As a Family Service Advocate and Early Literacy Professional Development Specialist advocating for children and families in Delaware; a first generational M. Ed graduate from Concordia University; a Human Services graduate from Springfield College. God has graced her with the ability to graciously be consistent in single parenting three beautiful children, having a career and taking back spiritual territory, with Godly authority by fire and by force! She has been at the forefront of building community programs, through grass-root efforts, that advocate for quality early care and education systems (ECE). The ECE workforce, early literacy, fought for societal changes for Delaware's impoverished communities struggling to overcome homelessness and food scarcity, and children and families facing various adversities of daily survival. As a Christian author and minister, it is Michelle's desire to minister to broken women, youth and children to mentor them in overcoming generational trauma and destroying generational curses. Michelle is a pioneer at the forefront of spiritual warfare prayer strategies, who desires through evangelism, healing, and deliverance, to share the Word of God and be a catalyst for societal justice, bringing hope and the knowledge of Christ's love to a lost world.

Prophetess Tréasa Brown was born and raised in the state of Colorado and is from a little city called Boulder. She's the 3rd child of four children and was dedicated back to the Lord as a child. Prophetess Brown was raised in the fear and admonition of the Lord and is a God-fearing Woman as a result. The Lord saved her in January of 2012, and she was filled with the Holy Ghost, March 28th of 2012. Prophetess Brown was baptized in April of 2016 under Brian Carn Ministries and that same year, baptized by her former Pastor, Superintendent Charles E. Scurles.

Prophetess Brown once served as a secretary in the Young Women's Christian Counsel. She was a primary Sunday school teacher, Local District Sunshine Band Leader, Bible Band Teacher, Assistant Coordinator, for the Young Women of Excellence, praise and worship leader, and has preached the Gospel. As a leader, Prophetess Tréasa Brown is currently serving under the Leadership of Pastor Larry Herron and First Lady Herron at DJIC Ministries, which stands for Deliverance Jesus Is Coming.

She loves spending time in the presence of God. She is a prayer warrior and intercessor. Prayer is her passion! Prophetess Brown was destined to be a writer, an author, and she is currently writing a book by the instruction of Almighty God titled, "Single Mothers and Living for Christ. She has journaled for seven years, writing prophetically while hearing, learning, and studying the voice of God. Prophetess Brown enjoys encouraging others and is drawn to the broken hearted. The Lord has called her to the nations, the prophetic ministry and to the Office of the Prophet. Prophetess Brown is yet to be birthed in the healing and deliverance ministry. The Lord is raising her up for His Glory! She has a hunger and a thirst for the things of God. She desires to please the Father that He will get the Glory out of her life! She's excited about what He is going to do, as her ministry is birthed! To God Be the Glory!

Melissa Jackson resides in Columbia, South Carolina. She has been in the midst of God and many Saints since the womb. Her mother is an evangelist and while pregnant, she evangelized to the surrounding neighborhood. At the tender age of 9, after reading the book of Revelation in one night, she made a conscious decision to give her life to Christ Jesus. From that night, she knew that life would never be the same. She immediately requested to be baptized in the bathtub of her home in Brooklyn, NY. She was raised to always read her Bible and pray every day so she can grow in the Lord and spread the gospel with confidence.

Melissa had many diverse roles in the ministry, such as Children Church Assistant, Church Program Coordinator, Drama Team Member, Choir Member, and Praise and Worship Team Member/Leader. She stays hungry and available with a humble heart to hear from God. Her passion is reading the Word of God, through the Spirit of God, and receiving downloads from heaven to teach and preach to those assigned to her.

ALLENA DOUGLAS BRATHWAITE is a humble servant of God. Allena is a speaker whose platform is telling others about God's grace, mercy, and wondrous miracles. Allena's passion is working in different outreach ministries sowing and providing essential items to the homeless, single mothers, teen mothers, sick and shut-in, and domestic violence victims. Allena is a woman who trusts God to bring her through real-life challenges—amazed by the wonder and faithfulness of God to do that and more. Her passion is to spread the word to whom has an ear to hear.

Allena believes her ministry thrives from the overflow because of her relationship with God and that she is a cheerful giver. I believe one should empower themselves to:

That our challenges Experience the Presence and power of God in their everyday life, trials are what builds our Christian Character by challenging our faith and teaching us to trust God fully.

We are Overcomers and are Victorious through our walk with Christ.

Look to Jesus, who is the hope and healer of all wounds.

Allena also knows what it is to hurt deeply. After losing her mother to an aneurysm and her grandmother gained her wings 12 hours later. She struggled with grief for 12 years and isolated herself from her home state of LA for 12 years. Allena found ultimate peace and healing by trusting God and his promises.

Allena is a Registered Nurse who has practiced for 30 years. Allena is currently working with The Army Behavior Health population. Her hard work, advocacy, and passion are reflected in all that she comes in contact with.

Allena is an advocate for domestic violence victims. She was formerly a charter member of The Liberty County Domestic Violence Task Force.

Allena is a Brain Aneurysm Survivor. Allena continually tells of others of her miraculous recovery. Allena is a strong advocate for brain aneurysm awareness. She is supportive to others through many platforms, and engages and lobbies legislators and congress to bring more awareness and funding for research.

ALLENA resides in Hinesville, GA, with her husband, Jose. Allena is the mother of 4 adult children, two stepdaughters, and has 12 grandchildren.

Tijuana Killian seeks to know the Lord more. She is pressing into Him for higher heights and deeper depths by focusing on His love that has pushed her beyond measures. She's a witnessing machine, captivating her audience. The grace of God is her friend, sticking closer than any brother. Reliance on the Spirit of truth to grow, her diligence was made for now. Her appointed time has come. She loves the Lord with all her heart, soul, mind, and strength.

Tijuana entered Ministry ready for battle. She has never backed down. Through many trials and tribulations, she stood her ground. Witnessing to the multitudes is her passion. She is seeking to save the lost by one comment at a time. She'll never be defeated, with God at her right hand, no doubt she has the victory. She is an overcomer by nature, unstoppable in the Spirit, a battle ram for the Lord, and heaven's defense mechanism. She's undefeated with multiple victories under her belt.

She once was blind, but now she sees. She once was lost, but now she's found. She is a prophet to the nations and God's mouthpiece. She has a right now word in her mouth for this dying generation. "Come back to me," are God's words coming out of her mouth. Repentance rings in her ears. She is sounding the alarm and moving towards her promise land.

Her goals and aspirations are to complete every God-ordained assignment in front of her. She is pressing towards the mark of the high calling. The calling on her life is to minister to the sick. She's double graced in this area. Multiple sicknesses tried to kill her, but God said no. She's here now for a reason. She is stable and sure of her redemption in Christ Jesus. Now is her set time for favor. Everything that the devil stole, God is giving it back to her.

Tijuana loves family, having fun, going out, dancing, singing, and being silly. Family dinners are one of her favorites. Her motives are pure. Family time is truly important to her. It represents the foundation of love and the gift of life. She adores her children, smiling from ear to ear at the sight of such anointed weapons of God. She knows God will use them mightly, sounding the alarm as well. Tijuana is the wife of her anointed husband, Gregory Killian. He is God's mouthpiece, as well. He is God's instrument in the earth. They have been married for nine years. Tijuana looks forward to this milestone, or ten year anniversary. It is a great accomplishment. She adores her husband and is so proud of the man he is becoming. She's fixed for this race—her eyes on the prize and faith.

References

1. History.com Editors, Dr. Martin Luther King, Jr. is assassinated, History, https://www.history.com/this-day-in-history/dr-king-is-assassinated. January 30, 2020.
2. Newton, John & Nazario, Susan. Police Say Seized Tapes Do No Incriminate Jackson: Investigation: Officials continue to interview children in connection with molestation allegations. LA Times, https://www.latimes.com/archives/la-xpm-1993-08-27-mn-28516-story.html. January 30, 2020
3. History.com Editors, "King of Pop" Michael Jackson dies at age 50, https://www.history.com/this-day-in-history/king-of-pop-michael-jackson-dies-at-age-50. January 30, 2020.
4. SI Staff (December 23, 2003). "Bryant distracted, scared amid sex assault case". Sports Illustrated. Associated Press. Archived from the original on September 6, 2004. Retrieved February 25, 2007.

5. Merriam-Webster.com Dictionary, s.v. "life," accessed March 1, 2020, https://www.merriam-webster.com/dictionary/life.
6. Corr, A. Kenneth. "What Does It Mean to Lead a Spiritual Life? A Christian Perspective," Explore Faith, 2002. Accessed March 2, 2020. http://www.explorefaith.org/steppingstones_SpiritualLife_Corr.htm
7. .Geggel, Laura (February 9, 2016) The Odds of Science. Live Science. February 15, 2020. Retrieved from: https://www.livescience.com/3780-odds-dying.html#deadlydiseases
8. Carteron, Nancy, MD. May 4, 2016. Lupus Outlook: How Does It Affect My Lifespan? Healthline. February 15, 2020. Retrieved from: http://www.healthline.com/health/lupus
9. Pastor, Buddy Dano. Anderson Bible Church. Death. The Bible Lists Seven Different Deaths. February 15, 2020. Retrieved from: www.divineviewpoint.com/death.pdf
10. Science Focus The Home of BBC Science Focus Magazine. February 15, 2020. Retrieved from: https://www.sciencefocus.com/science/how-many-ways-can-you-die/
11. Shola (2020) 7 Ways that People Actually Die Before They're Actually Dead. The Positivity Solution. Making Positivity the New Reality. February 15, 2020. Retrieved from: http://thepositivitysolution.com/7-ways-to-die/
12. Silver, Marc (December 18, 2014) NPR. Death Comes in Many Different Ways. And Some are a Bit Surprising. Goats and Soda Stories of Life in a Changing World. February 15, 2020. Retrieved from: https://www.npr.org/sections/goatsandsoda/2014/12/18/371486989/

death-comes-in-many-different-ways-and-some-are-a-bit-surprising

13. Bauckham, R. (1992). Hades, Hell. In D. N. Freedman (Ed.), The Anchor Yale Bible Dictionary (Vol. 3, p. 14). New York: Doubleday.
14. Miller L. Iron deficiency anemia: common and curable disease. Cold Spring Harb Perspect Med. 2012; a011866,
15. Photo 1: Normal Blood compared to Anemic Blood. https://sabeelhomeoclinic.com/what-is-anemia-symptoms-causes-diagnosis-and-homeopathic-treatment/ Accessed February 29, 2020
16. Photo 2: https://jrfibonacci.wordpress.com/2015/05/14/vanity-as-a-form-of-anxiety/
17. Iron-Deficiency Anemia. American Society of Hematology website. www.hematology.org/Patient /Anemia/Iron-Deficiency. Accessed February 29, 2020
18. Finberg KE. Unraveling mechanisms regulating systemic iron homeostasis. Hematology AM Soc Hematol Educ Program. 2011. Accessed February 29, 2020
19. Hemoglobin. MedlinePlus website. https://medlineplus.gov/ency/article//003645 November 21, 2016. Accessed February 29, 2020
20. Ferritin blood test. MedlinePlus website. https://medlineplus.gov/ency/article//003490.htm November 16, 2016, Accessed February 29, 2020
21. Medical definition of transferrin. Medice.net website www.medicinenet.com/script/main/art march 1, 2017. Accessed February 29, 2020

22. Heffernan, Katie. "Abortion Statistics," Springfield Right to Life, March 26, 2019. Accessed February 15, 2020, https://www.springfieldrtl.org/abortion-statistics/
23. Johnson, Shannon. January 5, 2016. Your Look Your Way. Varicose Vein Stripping. Healthline. February 15, 2020. Retrieved from: https://www.healthline.com/health/varicose-vein-stripping
24. Radiology Society of North America (RSNA) (2020). Varicose Vein Treatment (Endovenous Ablation of Varicose Veins). February 15, 2020. Retrieved from: https://www.radiologyinfo.org/en/info.cfm?pg=varicoseabl
25. National Blood Clot Alliance. Stop the Clot. Signs and Symptoms. February 15, 2020. Retrieved from: https://www.stoptheclot.org/blood-clot-information/blood-clots-in-the-united-states/
26. Brain Aneurysm Foundation. https://bafound.org
27. "Sudden Unexpected Infant Death and Sudden Infant Death Syndrome." CDC. https://www.cdc.gov/sids/data.htm (Accessed February 2, 2020).
28. The National Child Traumatic Stress Network (NCTSN) Retrieved from: https://www.nctsn.org/what-is-child-trauma/about-child-trauma
29. "Systemic lupus erythematosus," Medline, Accessed February 28, 2020, https://medlineplus.gov/ency/article/000435.htm
30. "Systemic Lupus Erythematosus (SLE)," Healthline, Accessed February 28, 2020, https://www.healthline.com/health/systemic-lupus-erythematosus

31. "Lupus," Mayo Clinic, 2017, Accessed February 28, 2020, https://www.mayoclinic.org/diseases-conditions/lupus/symptoms-causes/syc-20365789

32. Patel, Rasna. "A Case of Lupus Cerebritis," Healio, 2018, Accessed February 28, 2020, https://www.healio.com/psychiatry/journals/psycann/2018-7-48-7/%7B9d542dd3-055b-4622-9e36-09039e204217%7D/a-case-of-lupus-cerebritis

33. "Cerebellar Stroke," Healthline, Accessed February 28, 2020, https://www.healthline.com/health/cerebellar-stroke

Index

A

abortion, 34, 47, 94–95, 136
abortion statistics, 91
abuse, domestic, 179
advancements, 41
adversities, 226
affliction, 157
afterlife, 63
age, 28, 36, 87, 98, 102, 132, 158, 175, 190, 225, 234
Airborne diseases, 45
alarm, 233
album, 116
Alcohol, 45
ambition, 26, 143
angels, 136, 145, 153
anger, 56, 131
animal patrol, 201

anointing, 91
apartments, 143, 170
Apostle, 220
aspirations, 87, 232
atmosphere, 151
attacks, 148, 190, 196, 200

B

bandages, 100, 106
barriers, 125, 223
behavior, 144, 168, 209
believers, 7, 28, 35, 50
benefits, 32, 37–38, 85
Bible, 4, 6, 33, 55, 58, 66, 73, 82, 109, 117, 119–20, 142, 160, 182
Bible Lists, 48
birth control, 76
bites, 99, 200
blessing, 33, 36, 59, 65, 109, 213
blood, 10, 22, 38, 65, 91, 94, 98, 103, 156
blood clots, 97, 101, 104–5, 199
blood disease, 46
blood flow, 98
blood levels, 103
bloodstream, 72
blood vessel, 192
body, 37–38, 41–42, 44, 46, 56, 59, 71–73, 80, 83, 98, 104, 120, 122, 190, 192
bondage, 68

brain, 75, 98, 188, 192
Brain Aneurysm Foundation, 109, 111, 237
bruises, 146–47, 155
Bryant, Kobe, 29–30
businesses, 75, 216, 219

C

Catholic mass, 30
celebrities, 2, 5, 25, 27, 29–30
cell, 207
Chemical toxins, 46
Chest pain, 84
Childbirth, 47
children, 29, 34, 36, 51, 145, 147, 149, 158, 160–62, 201, 211, 215, 225–26
child-trauma, 161
Christ Jesus, 56, 229, 233
cirrhosis, 3, 46
cloud, 129
clubs, 116, 140, 174–76
college, 144, 219
commandment, 18, 49, 73
condemnation, 68
confinement, 207
confirmation, 172
constipation, 158
contractions, 90, 96
control, 30, 34, 85, 120, 145, 181
conviction, 130–31

Coronavirus, 45
cough, 127, 133, 137
countenance, 148
couple, 99, 105, 121, 162, 164–66, 170, 176, 179, 189, 210
courage, 26, 57
creation, 34, 64, 66, 221
Crib Death, 132
cycle, 73, 98

D

darkness, 26, 53, 56, 63, 66, 96, 124, 156, 196
dark secret, 27
dark times, 196
daughter, 168, 170
dead body, 32
dead spirit, 42
death, 2–3, 10, 12, 28–31, 42–43, 48–53, 56, 62–63, 69, 87–89, 114, 127–28, 153, 160, 186
deathbeds, 3
Declarations, 9
decree, 11, 14, 16, 18–20, 23
deliverance, 38, 171, 226
deliverance ministry, 216
depths, 23, 152
destination, 29
destinies, 27, 93–94, 96, 135, 204
deteriorate, 188
devil, 3, 7, 26, 94, 96, 126, 135–36, 138, 158, 162, 180, 190–92, 196, 205, 210

devil's job, 124
devotion, 55, 57
diseases, 33, 188, 190
disobedience, 52, 114
disobedient, 50, 201
divorce, 149, 208, 211
doctors, 3, 84–85, 87, 90, 98–100, 103, 188–89, 192, 199
dominion, 64
dreams, 41, 87, 129, 136, 171, 223
drowning, 151, 206
drugs, 28
dysfunction, 160

E

ear, 230, 233
emotional responses, 161
energy, 73, 81–82, 155
equality, 26
escape, 41–42, 139, 197
eternity, 33, 61, 122
everlasting, 69
evil, 15, 49, 78, 95, 104, 135
ex-boyfriend, 116, 120
ex-girlfriends, 171, 178
Exodus, 26, 35, 134–35, 157
expectation, 35
experience, 5, 36, 82, 161, 211

F

faith, 7, 79, 111, 121, 230, 233
faithfulness, 230
families, 12, 29, 38, 66, 76, 108, 120, 165, 167, 205, 210, 215, 219, 226, 233
family dinners, 233
family members, 102, 166
Famous Deaths, 25
fasting, 40, 203
father, 9–10, 13, 23, 28, 68, 81, 88, 94, 117, 126, 136, 153
fibroids, 154–55, 157–59
fight, 26, 128, 179, 196
fish, 3, 64
flaps, 98
flood, 65
Flowers, 57
forehead, 120, 155
forgive, 13
forgive people, 31
foundation, 88, 161, 223
freedom, 26, 38, 207
frontal region, 111
fruit, 51
fun, 132, 233

G

generational curses, 161, 226
generational trauma, 226
Genesis, 54

giver, 157–58
glasses, 119, 140, 179
globe, 34, 217
glory, 34, 54–57, 67, 88–89, 93, 114, 184, 204, 210, 213, 228
gold, 26, 57
Good News, 51
gospel, 116, 126, 216, 227
grace, 52, 65–66, 69, 106, 230
grace of God, 202, 232
grandchildren, 110, 231
grandmother, 147, 230
grass, 119, 123
grave, 42, 53
greatness, 91–92, 96
grief, 111, 158
grim reaper, 140
growth, 90, 213
guilt, 66, 68
gun violence, 174, 179

H

hair, 115
hallway, 94, 115, 140
happiness, 28, 73
Hay Fever, 134
Headaches, 84
healing, 157, 171, 226, 231
health, 12, 73, 85, 181, 199
heart, 56–57, 98, 103, 115, 130, 136, 171, 199, 220

heart attack, 44
heart disease, 44
heart doctor, 98
heart patients, 192
heart rate, 192
heaven, 1, 4, 55–57, 59–60, 64, 66, 68, 122, 156, 229
heights, 23, 232
hell, 4, 21, 42–43, 60, 62–63, 199, 236
Hematology, 72
hemoglobin, 72, 80, 82, 85, 236
holy, 40, 147
Holy Ghost, 129
holy nation, 66
home, 26, 28, 48, 74, 147, 149, 164, 167–68, 170, 174, 200, 229
homeless, 166, 230
homelessness, 223, 226
Homicide, 44
hospital, 102, 119–20, 122, 187–88, 224
house, 115, 117, 120, 137, 140–41, 168–70, 201, 210, 215
households, 143, 146
humanity, 50–52, 65
hungry, 75, 137
Hurricane, 46
hurting, 170, 204, 221
husband, 88, 143–44, 146–49, 209

I

idol, 27, 210

immortal beings, 69
immune system, 188
immunosuppressant, 189
impatient, 160, 167
infants, 2, 134, 137
infertility, 158
inheritance, 34
instincts, 133, 137, 142
instruction, 4, 66, 227
intercession, 60, 217
intercessors, 227
iron, 71–73
Iron-Deficiency Anemia, 72
iron pills, 76

J

Jesus, 9–23, 28, 57, 60–61, 65, 67–68, 114, 117, 124, 129–31, 134, 136, 142, 147–48, 196
Jewish writers, 63
Joseph, 136
judgment, 50, 65
jumping, 47, 206

K

kindness, 197
kingdom, 15, 26–27, 35, 92–93, 96, 135, 159, 213, 219–20
Kingdom-minded, 223
kingdom principles, 52, 219

L

laws, 2, 51–52
leaders, 25, 227
leadership, 26, 220
legacy, 29, 34, 136
legs, 80, 97–100, 104–6
lessons, 5, 25, 28–30, 162
lethargy, 188, 191
lifetime, 41–42, 73
liver transplant, 3
lungs, 72–73, 101, 199
lupus, 47, 188–90
Lupus/Stroke, 187
lusts, 94, 160, 182

M

Malaria, 45
Malaysia, 2
malicious plan, 136
Malnourishment, 45
manifestation, 220
mansion, 27, 59
marital vows, 29
marriage, 205, 219, 221
married couples, 219
married students, 143
meat, 127, 159

median, 123
medication, 103, 189
medicine, 41, 103, 192
Meditations, 208
memories, 36, 63, 190
Meningitis, 46
mentor, 36, 226
mentor people, 223
mercy, 52, 65–66, 69, 106, 186, 211, 220, 230
mighty tool, 220
milky drug, 27
minister, 209, 220, 226, 232
ministry, 161, 216–17, 225, 229–30
miraculous, 67, 217
miraculous recovery, 231
miraculous signs, 109
money, 28, 143, 174–76, 182
Moses, 134–36, 216
mother, 78, 88–92, 96, 120, 128, 133, 137, 144, 153, 196, 215, 229–30
mother-in-law, 144
mountains, 29, 34
movie, 200
mucus, 133
murderer, 94

N

NAME of HELL, 62
natural disasters, 66

natural rebellion, 52
nature, 50–51
negative words, 215
neurological deficits, 109
New Testament, 222
nose, 27, 133–34

O

office, 176, 220, 228
organs, 188, 190
overdose, 2, 206
overtime, 107
oxygen, 73, 80, 98

P

pain, 56, 59, 69, 90, 95, 98, 100, 119, 155, 204, 211
parenting, 143
parents, 51, 115, 117, 120, 133–34, 137, 160–61
Parkinson's disease, 45
passion, 50, 227, 229–31
patience, 211
patients, 3, 28, 101, 110, 181, 188
peace, 26, 28, 55, 137–38, 171, 204, 210
peers, 29, 97, 132, 134
persecution, 23
perspective, 36, 223
Physical life, 33
pictures, 63, 165

platforms, 152, 230–31
police, 27, 145, 147, 179, 201
police officers, 145
possessive, 143
power, 7, 10, 23, 35, 50, 120, 122, 125, 142, 156, 196, 215, 230
pray, 7, 57, 60, 129, 138, 197, 209
prayer life, 107, 144, 163
prayers, 7, 69, 167, 197, 208, 217, 227
prayer warrior, 227
praying, 5, 77, 125, 171
preach, 35, 134, 167, 219, 229
precious opportunity, 67
prednisone, 189
pregnancy, 87, 90
prescriptions, 77
principalities, 23, 156
process, 31, 89, 94, 98, 181, 183, 213
productivity, 172
prophecy, 136, 138
Prophetic, 218
propofol, 27–28
prosperous, 18, 38
protection, 161

R

radio, 112, 204
Rapture, 41
RBCs, 72–73

redemption, 66, 233
regrets, 3, 68
relationship, 53, 140, 144, 165, 172, 175–76, 182, 230
religious spirit, 125
Respiratory Therapy, 28
restoration, 52, 66
resurrection, 6–7, 69
retribution, 63
righteousness, 15
royal priesthood, 66
rubber band, 176
rulers, 50, 156

S

sacrifice, 153
safety, 2, 123
salvation, 6, 57, 60, 150
sea, 42, 64
seat belt, 161
seeds, 116
self-esteem, 181
sensation, 211
set time, 233
severity, 158
sex, 116, 142, 179, 182
   oral, 177
sexual acts, 177
sexual preferences, 27
shadow, 56, 68, 113, 186

shortcomings, 182
shoulders, 115, 180
shrink, 158–59
sinners, 35, 42
sinuses, 133–34
sinus problems, 132
sister, 56, 77, 102, 117, 119, 128–29, 209
sleep, 37, 41, 77, 83, 100, 103, 137, 139, 172, 177, 181, 183, 195–96, 200, 209
smoking, 97, 99, 106
snake, 200–201
social media, 171, 204
souls, 4, 35, 41, 53, 63, 69, 122, 159
species, 34
Spiritual Life, 33
stars, 66, 136
stomach, 168, 189
storms, 162
strength, 57, 104, 232
stress, 21, 37, 73
strip club, 115
stripper, 139, 142
stroke, 3, 190, 194
suicidal, 203–4
suicide, 2, 16, 66, 203–6
suicide ward, 207
supernatural, 125, 135
supplies, 35
surgery, 106
surrender, 161

survival, 111
symptoms, 74, 85, 101, 105, 155, 159, 187, 193

T

teachers, 35, 214
Tears, 56
technology, 35, 41
Terrorism, 47
Terrorized, 154
texting, 3, 124, 169
threat, 26, 96, 135, 153
tissues, 60, 72–73, 190
tongue irritations, 74
tongues, 74–75, 91, 120, 125, 215
Tornado, 46
tournaments, 29
toxic people, 40
traffic, 119, 169, 179
transgression, 50
treasures, 11, 68
tricks, 176–77
truth, 94, 114, 126, 180–81, 204, 211, 232

U

uncle, 213–14

V

vacations, 36, 165
Vaccines, 45
Varicose Vein Treatment, 98
vehicle, 118–19, 123, 128, 178
victims, 165, 179
victory, 56, 59–60, 114, 213, 232
violence, 26, 45, 65–66
virus, 188
voice, 121, 126, 186, 208, 215, 227
Volcanic eruption, 46
vomiting, 161, 191

W

War battles, 47
warning signs, 131, 141–42, 203
water, 6, 38, 151–52
weaknesses, 68, 74, 84
wealthy place, 59
weapons, 138, 145, 212
wisdom, 36, 40, 57, 209, 213
woke, 117, 139, 142, 155–56, 170, 198
woman, 64, 67, 142, 170, 230
womb, 34, 89, 94–95
workout, 99
world, 26–27, 29, 50–51, 53, 60, 64–65, 67, 121, 128, 131, 156, 159, 210, 213, 216
worship, 136, 157